HOW TO BE
CONFIDENT
AND ASSERTIVE
AT WORK

Suzanne and Conrad Potts

A HOW TO BOOK

ROBINSON

ROBINSON

First published in Great Britain in 2010 as *Entitled to Respect* by How To Books

This edition published in 2015 by Robinson

7 9 10 8 6

A CIP catalogue record for this book is available from the British Library.

ISBN: 978-1-84528-596-8

Typeset in Great Britain by Ian Hughes, www.mousematdesign.com
Printed and bound by CPI Group (UK) Ltd, Croydon, CR0 4YY

Papers used by Robinson are from well-managed forests and other responsible sources

MIX
Paper from
responsible sources
FSC® C104740

Robinson
An imprint of
Little, Brown Book Group
Carmelite House
50 Victoria Embankment
London EC4Y 0DZ

An Hachette UK Company
www.hachette.co.uk

www.littlebrown.co.uk

How To Books are published by Robinson, an imprint of Little, Brown Book Group. We welcome proposals from authors who have first-hand experience of their subjects. Please set out the aims of your book, its target market and its suggested contents in an email to Nikki.Read@howtobooks.co.uk

*"Assertion is not about being liked,
it's about being respected."*

Contents

Part 2 – **WORK SITUATIONS**

A step-by-step guide in how to deal with some of the most common
situations that you face during your working life.

INTRODUCTION

"No one will give you respect unless you give it to yourself."

Conrad has never laid claim to being a good driver. A litany of accidents and insurance claims over a number of years bear witness to that. It's not that Conrad is deliberately uncaring or selfish on the road; indeed he's often courteous and respectful to his fellow road users. However, what sometimes happens to him may well happen to you and many other motorists.

Just imagine: you're driving down the road when seemingly out of nowhere someone selfishly barges in front of you, pushing in and causing you to take drastic action or almost have an accident.

Typically there follows a barrage of insults, much blowing of horns and the exchange of a few extravagant expletives. Sometimes you, the 'wronged', may pursue the other driver aggressively gesticulating in an unfriendly manner or sit there in the car fuming and hurling further abuse, venting your anger.

At the end of all of this, you may notice your blood pressure has risen considerably, you may be trembling or sweating, but will certainly be in a state of hyper-tension and ill-humour. The rest of the day is now affected by this event and the cat had better find a new hiding place when you come home.

How we respond – 'stimulus and response'

In such situations you unknowingly lose out in a number of ways. If you ever take the time to stop and reflect on what happened, you may conclude that you were just like a puppet on a string, controlled by someone else's behaviour, responding *reactively* to whatever they did as if you had no influence over what you said and did.

Driving demonstrates to us one of the most important lessons we have learned in life – that we are responsible for our own feelings, behaviour and actions. The more we are able to put a 'gap' between what psychologists call 'stimulus and response', the more we are able to choose what we want and the less we feel manipulated or in the grip of something or someone else. Sometimes it is a hard pill to swallow but we always have a choice – and every choice has its own set of implications.

So, in the situation we described where Conrad reacted aggressively, he lost out in many ways:

- He was no longer in control of his own behaviour – somebody else was.
- He was reactive and on the back foot all the time.
- He was angry, in a bad mood and allowed the feelings to persist for the rest of the day.
- His blood pressure rose to a unhealthy level.
- And he didn't feel proud and good about himself.

Do you feel you come out of similar situations with your self-respect intact or do you feel you have let yourself down in some way?

To paraphrase Mahatma Ghandi, "No one can take away your self-respect unless you give it away yourself." You need to respect yourself first and behave in a way that is congruent with that behaviour. When you can respect yourself and persistently act accordingly, you manifest every possibility that someone else will respect you.

Initiating the gap (or pause)

When you behave in a reactive mode to situations like this you begin to teach yourself a pattern of behaviour. You behave as though there is no gap between stimulus and response and the result is a feeling of having 'lost out' and gradually a sense of losing your self-respect.

What you need to do is 'cut the puppet strings' and place *a gap* between the stimulus, e.g. being 'wronged', and the response, e.g. your subsequent anger. The magic of creating that gap is immense. When you give yourself the right to 'pause' (the *gap*), you create choice.

You *may* then choose to rant or rave, in which case you will probably enjoy it more! Or you may choose to quieten yourself so you don't suffer high blood pressure, etc.

You can choose to have different thoughts about the person or the situation. And at the end of it all, you are considerably more likely to maintain your self-respect and act in a way that will be more helpful in this and other stressful situations. You teach yourself a different pattern.

Our intention in this book is to offer you many practical ideas that will give you choice that you can use in the gap. Initiating a gap takes a second or two – who says you have to react instantly? The more you practise creating the gap, the quicker and easier it becomes to act in a self-empowering way.

Our belief is that as human beings we are sovereign people and that our birthright entitles us to make our own unique choices. By accepting that you can put a gap between stimulus and response, you acknowledge that you are responsible for your own choices: no one can make you do or feel anything . . . happy . . . sad . . . angry . . . foolish . . . unless you choose to allow it.

You can no longer blame other people for what you do, e.g. "You made me do X or Y". You have, at some level, made a choice to allow another to affect you in whatever way they have.

This harsh reality sets you free from others' control or manipulation and allows you to shape your own tomorrow.

How you choose to read this book

You will find in this book a number of challenging work situations that most of us will have experienced at some point. If you choose to, you can treat this like a recipe book and go directly to those areas where you think you need most support and find an entire recipe of helpful ideas. We offer a number of choices and techniques for you to use and we leave you to work with the ones that feel right for you.

At the heart of what we suggest is the notion of integrity, authenticity and respect for you and others. Where you can find a solution that maintains the dignity and respect of all concerned, you are more likely to achieve a long-lasting result that all parties can sign up to.

Part 1 of this book, **The Toolbox**, provides you with an explanation of the tools and techniques that underpin your assertion and provides you with a strong foundation from which to work.

After each tool has been explained, together with examples, you have an opportunity to practise your skill in them by completing an exercise and then getting a response of what we believe to be the best answer.

In **Part 2** of this book, **Work Situations**, we offer a number of ways to deal with specific situations. **Chapters 12–26** are designed to help you like a recipe book would and if you follow the sequence suggested in these chapters, you will be doing the most appropriate things to bring about the 'best' result.

Work can be the most fulfilling time of your life – you're likely to spend up to two-thirds of it at work. By adopting many of the ideas in this book, you have the personal power to bring that fulfilment about.

However you choose to use this material we wish you every success as you progress to create a world where you achieve more of what you want in your working life and gain the respect you're entitled to.

Suzanne and Conrad Potts

PART 1

THE TOOLBOX

The tools and techniques
– helpful things you need to know
about before you start your journey
to becoming more confident
and assertive at work

CHAPTER 1
BEHAVIOURAL FLEXIBILITY

You and I can persist with actions and behaviours long after they have become useful or helpful. Some of us know no other way, even though we are aware that what we're doing isn't working. These repetitive behaviours soon become habits, which calcify and prevent us from being flexible in our response to life's daily challenges.

A reminder of our stubborn resistance to change can be summed up as follows:

> "If you always do what you have always done
> You'll always get what you've always got."

In **Part 1** of this book we offer you a number of tools and techniques that will contribute to your flexibility and help you make different choices with different results. All the tools and techniques have been validated in the cauldron of real-life experience and we offer them to you because many people who have attended our various training programmes have proved they work.

Different choices and different levels of change

As you will see from **Figure 1.1,** when you want to make changes in what you think, what you do and what you say, you can do so at various levels.

For instance, if you wanted to develop aspects of your *non-verbal behaviour (body language)* the changes are less fundamental to the core of who you are and can be done pretty immediately. If you change your body language, e.g. give firmer direct eye contact, you won't change your personality or deeper elements that make you uniquely you.

If you choose to change an *unhelpful belief*, you will change something more fundamental about yourself. When you take on a new *belief* authentically, with full commitment, the changes will also influence your concept of *rights, self- talk, verbal and non-verbal behaviour.*

Figure 1.1

Beliefs

Rights and responsibilities

Self-talk

**Non-verbal behaviour (body language)
and verbal behaviour**

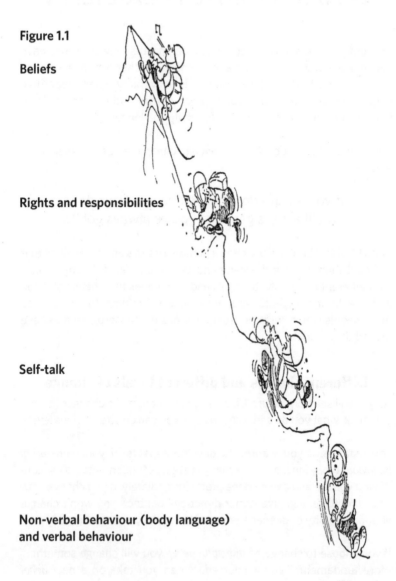

Choosing to change and master any one of these levels will increase your flexibility and increase your chances of achieving the best results with people.

It is wise to master these levels one by one in your own time and experience how successful they can be. Boosted by your success you can take another tool out of the **Toolbox** and get that to work for you as well – *one thing at a time and little and often* will work best with behavioural change.

Remember to be kind to yourself as you reflect on how well you have applied a new idea or technique. The real success is in wholeheartedly trying something new. Use self-analysis and feedback like a directional compass to tell you where you are, get you where you want to be and if necessary what you need to do to get back on course. You may not succeed fully the first time, but remember research shows that it takes at least 30 days' persistent repetition before any skill is internalised and feels natural to you.

If you are not relying on other people to deliver what you want in life, you are left with yourself as a resource. What you achieve will happen by releasing the enormous potential you have through your own personal power, self-belief and inter-personal skills. There are many models of inter-personal effectiveness. We believe assertion is one of the most powerful ways of achieving the best results with people because at the centre of assertion is a belief system focused on how we respect ourselves and others.

We have run many hundreds of workshops on assertion and by far the most frequent question asked by delegates is, "How do I gain respect at work?" By the end of our workshops people are very clear about what *they* need to do to gain respect.

Change comes from *within* first and from deciding to make different choices. The aim of this book is to help you build behavioural flexibility and make assertive choices to achieve the results you want at work.

CHAPTER 2

WHAT IS ASSERTION?

Definitions of assertive, non-assertive and aggressive behaviour

Before we go any further, here's our view of what assertion is about.

There are many definitions of the word 'assertion'. Indeed, often people attend a programme either having been sent by their boss 'to get more of their own way' or to be more 'aggressive'. Yet it is one of the paradoxes of life that attending to others' needs helps you achieve more of your own.

Assertion is about behaviour and not people. All of us behave in all three ways – in some situations we can behave aggressively or non-assertively – but that does not mean we are aggressive *people* or non-assertive *people*.

Assertive behaviour is when you stand up for your own rights in a way that does not violate the rights of others – 'Rights' are a key element of assertiveness. A right is something to which you are justly entitled and for which you don't have to ask somebody else's permission.

Assertion leads to an honest, open and direct expression of your point of view, which, at the same time, shows that you understand the other person's position. It is based on the belief that you have needs to be met and so do others and the most effective approach is to find a way in which both parties achieve sufficient of what they want – *win:win*.

Aggressive behaviour is when you stand up for your own rights in such a way that you ignore or dismiss the rights of another. You express your thoughts, feelings and views in unsuitable ways, because you may honestly believe your views to be right.

Aggression enhances you at the expense of others and puts others down. It is based on the belief that your opinions are more important than those of others. It is characterised by blaming, by showing contempt, disregard, hostility, and by attacking or patronising others' views and ideas.

Non-assertive behaviour is when you don't stand up for your rights or you stand up for them in such a way that you make it easy for others to ignore or override them. You express your thoughts, feelings and beliefs in often apologetic, cautious or self-effacing ways. You may fail to express your views or feelings altogether.

Non-assertion is based on the belief that your own needs and wants are not as important as other people's and that it will take too much unpleasantness and conflict to realise them. You can be apologetic and submissive in standing up for your needs and wants, or stand up for them in a manipulative and less authentic way.

Typical of submissive behaviour are long, rambling, justifying explanations often putting ourselves down while attempting to accommodate the needs and views of others.

Examples of aggressive, assertive and non-assertive behaviours

You have been asked by your boss to take on an additional task, which involves taking responsibility for some of your colleagues' work. You feel reluctant to do this because you have not been given the authority or the resources to make a success of the task.

After the first couple of weeks you are behind schedule and your boss phones you up to check how everything is going.

Here are three different responses you might give:

An aggressive response:
"It's a waste of time. You've put me in a very awkward situation and taken advantage of my willingness to help. You've just dropped me in it and it's no surprise that we are behind schedule!"

A non-assertive response:
"Oh . . . um things seem to be ok, perhaps . . . some minor difficulties here and there. You know . . . you'd expect that . . . I guess. Things could be better, but I'm sure we'll get there eventually."

An assertive response:
"I am finding it difficult to redirect people's efforts when I haven't the authority to do so. Now I've been doing the job for a couple of weeks I think we need to sit down and discuss exactly what support I need. When can we do that?"

Exercise 2.1: HOW ASSERTIVE ARE YOU?

An important first step in increasing your assertion is to identify how much assertion you currently use when you're at work.

Part 1
The question we'd like you to think about is:

When you're at work what proportion of the time do you behave:

- assertively? ....%
- non-assertively? ....%
- aggressively? ....%

Part 2
At this point you might consider: in what work situations do you find it most difficult to behave assertively?

1. What's the situation?
2. Who are the people involved?
3. What is the usual result?
4. What would you like to happen next time? Visualise the best outcome (see Chapter 5 Visualisation).
5. Is this a win:win? (See Chapter 9 Win:win Outcomes.)

CHAPTER 3

OUR VERBAL BEHAVIOUR

The impression we make on others

There are various points of view about how long it takes to make a first impression. Untrained interviewers notoriously seem to make up their minds as to whether they like or dislike a candidate very quickly; anything, it seems, from 45 to 90 seconds. Interviewers then spend the rest of the time validating their instinctive choice – their gut feeling.

If you cast your mind back to when you last went for a job interview, you will probably be curious about what it is you can do in 45–90 seconds that makes such an impression. You can walk into the room, say "Hello", sit down, reply to a few non-controversial questions and niceties, look the interviewer in the eye, or not, and hope above hope that you are being perceived as cool, calm and collected – just what they are looking for!

What then is the interviewer picking up in those first early exchanges?

A large part of the impression you have made will have come from 'what you say', 'how you say it' and your overall presence conveyed by your 'body language'. In Chapter 4 we will look at the impact your body language has on the perception of others, but first of all let us look at the words and phrases you use that give others a sense of what kind of person you are.

The following language examples signify to others that your behaviour is aggressive, non-assertive or assertive. We'll start with words and phrases that are associated with aggressive behaviour.

Aggressive language patterns

Attacking
"You should be more considerate!"

Excessive use of 'I' statements
"I don't think that is the right way to go about this."

Expressing opinion as fact
"Everyone agrees this is how it happens."

Concentrating on your needs and disregarding others
"I have to have this work done now or I won't make the deadline."

Blaming
"If others worked as conscientiously as I do we wouldn't be in this mess."

Threatening
"If you can't work the extra hours as a goodwill gesture, we won't be able to consider you as someone who goes the extra mile for us."

Using 'ought', 'should', 'must'
"You must agree that I am correct on this one."

Exaggerating
"You always seem to forget."

Denigrating
"You've produced a rubbish piece of work."

Manipulating
"If you cared about my situation, you wouldn't do that."

Let's now look at words and phrases that are associated with non-assertive behaviour.

Non-assertive language patterns

Tentative and reluctant agreement
"Well, perhaps it would be all right."

Hinting at doubts
"Oh, I don't know what the boss would say."

Unwilling to state a preference
"I don't really mind. I'll have whatever you're having."

Moaning or complaining

"Not another managerial initiative. Why can't they get it right?"

Fishing for praise, help or support

"It's not that expensive so I suppose it doesn't look that good. What do you think?"

Seeking approval and permission

"Do you think I can really just go up to her and ask her?"

Self-pity

"I always get the most difficult things to do."

Self-effacing

"I'm hopeless at handling this kind of problem."

Suggestions at your expense

"I am so busy . . . I don't know whether I am coming or going . . . but leave it with me and I'll fit it in somehow."

Building others up at your own expense

"You are so much better at this than I am."

Long, rambling sentences

"I'd really like to help you if I could but you know how it is; we don't really have enough time to do even the basic things well and then there is all the extra work people expect you to do without giving you any of the resources and so you can see it's not easy . . ."

And finally let's see some words and phrases that are associated with assertive behaviour.

Assertive language patterns

'I' language indicating ownership of ideas, views and feelings

"I want us in the future to work directly with each other and I think we can then get the best results."

Direct self-expression of your thoughts and feelings
"When you cancel meetings at very short notice, it causes credibility problems for us and I feel really annoyed."

Stating what you want
"I'd like us to sit down and work this out so we do not repeat the same mistakes again."

Focus on specific behaviour and facts instead of opinions
"Joan, I noticed how everyone understood the graphs in your presentation. They all commented how it made the unintelligible easy to understand. Thank you."

Clarity
"Thanks for asking me. I can't help you at this time. I've already got more than I can handle to complete by Friday."

Brief – 'less is more'
"I would like a chance to say something."

Allowing others to choose for themselves
"I'd like to appoint this person. How do you feel?"

Questioning, particularly open questions
"What, why, where, who, when, how?"

Distinguishing opinion from fact
"In my view, we have to ask the question before we act."

Silence, once you have stated your opinion
". . . and that is why I think this is the best option to use."

Focus on what can be done
"How about we speak to Pete and Natasha and get their ideas?"

Exercise 3.1: LANGUAGE OF ASSERTION, NON-ASSERTION AND AGGRESSION

You're a 'fly on the wall' at a discussion between three people at a team meeting. Kate, the team leader, is having one of her catch-ups with Tracey and Zak. Can you spot when they are being assertive, non-assertive or aggressive just by the words used?

Is this assertive, non-assertive or aggressive?

1. Kate
*"Zak, I'm unsure where this is taking us.
What exactly do you see as the issue here?"* ....

2. Zak
*"Don't you realise I'm up to my neck in
problems? How can you ask me that now?"* ....

3. Tracey
*"Zak, can I ask what the real problem
is so we can put together a plan to help you?"* ....

4. Zak
*"If you really wanted to help you'd just let me get
on with doing my job and not keep calling these
stupid meetings."* ....

5. Kate
*"I appreciate you're extremely busy.
I see our meetings differently. I believe they give us a
chance to re-adjust priorities and help each other."* ....

6. Zak
*"Well, I don't! And I'm sure no one else does.
What about you, Tracey?"* ....

7. Tracey
"Perhaps ... I don't know ... sometimes they are

a good idea. Other times ... well ...
it's always good to get
together, isn't that right, Kate?"

8. Zak
"Well, I'd like to know how long this one will take
and whether it will be the usual waste of time?"

9. Kate
"Zak, what will make this meeting useful for you
and how much time can you spare?"

10. Tracey
"I think putting a time on our 'get together' will be helpful.
I also have deadlines to meet. What about another
20 minutes?"

11. Kate
"Twenty minutes won't solve anything. Surely, you two
can give it more time? After all, these meetings
are for your benefit."

12. Zak
"Look, I'm sorry. It's just I could have done without
this meeting today. If we could do it after work I could
give it more time."

13. Kate
"I wouldn't normally have a problem, only today
I have to get to my daughter's school on time."

14. Tracey
"Me too. Sorry, I don't know if I can: I'm not sure
I'll have time to change my arrangements.
I'd really like to but it's difficult at the moment
and anyway my car's got problems and I was hoping
to have to maybe take it to the garage. Sorry."

15. Kate
*"In that case, I suggest we spend 20 minutes
on Zak's most important issue and then meet again
tomorrow at the same time."*   ....

16. Zak
*"Oh, can't we postpone our meeting for a couple of
days? I mean I have an important presentation to
prepare for and I promised my team I might help
them with it if I could."*   ....

17. Tracey
*"Let's get started so we can make the most of the
20 minutes."*   ....

Answer to Exercise 3.1

Kate	**Assertive** – open question asking for information.
Zak	**Aggressive** – attacking and blaming.
Tracey	**Assertive** – appropriate use of 'I' language when speaking for herself and 'we' language when it referred to putting a plan together.
Zak	**Aggressive** – a continuation of the theme started at 2.
Kate	**Assertive** – first showing empathy for Zak's position, stating her own view on the meetings and reasons for the meeting.
Zak	**Aggressive** – still with the 'red mist' – claiming opinion as though it were fact.
Tracey	**Non-assertive** – we are unclear as to what Tracey really does think. She certainly is expressing it in a vague way and then looks to Kate for permission to hold that view.

Zak	**Aggressive** – Zak's moving towards assertion but it's spoilt by the last bit – an accusatory generalisation.
Kate	**Assertive** – seeking a resolution, finding out others' needs and looking to find a win:win result.
Tracey	**Assertive** – picking up the theme of win:win, stating her view on her workload and suggesting a option.
Kate	**Aggressive** – perhaps becoming frustrated but nevertheless becoming accusatory, blaming and irritated.
Zak	**Assertive** – apologising for the manner of his outbursts and offering an option.
Kate	**Assertive** – stating a personal problem in a positive way and giving what seems a truthful reason.
Tracey	**Non-assertive** – plenty of excuses but which one is the real reason, if any?
Kate	**Assertive** – making a proposal, offering a possible win:win.
Zak	**Non-assertive** – this time it seems it's Zak's turn to hedge his bets and not come out with the real reason.
Tracey	**Assertive** – making a suggestion with a benefit for all.

(As an aside, we're not at the catch-up meeting so we don't know how it progressed and whether they parked the issue of 'how useful' the meetings are to another time. If Kate does not face up to this issue at some point she is being non-assertive with her team.)

CHAPTER 4

NON-VERBAL BEHAVIOUR

The prisoner in the dock looked distinctly uncomfortable as the prosecuting lawyer slowly approached. The trial for murder was grinding to a conclusion and this was the final interrogation. In a slow deliberate voice the prosecuting lawyer looked deep and long into the prisoner's face and said, "Can you look me in the eyes and tell me you did not commit this heinous murder?" and waited for his answer.

The prisoner in the dock took several seconds, averted his eyes and looked down. In a determined voice and shaking his head he replied, "No! I didn't do it, you gotta believe me."

Subsequently, a unanimous jury found the defendant guilty of first degree murder. When some of the jurors were later asked why they were so sure of the defendant's guilt they cited circumstantial evidence and several of them highlighted the moment when the defendant averted his eyes and looked down when the crucial question was asked.

This is a true story, reported a few years ago in the *New York Times*. The defendant appealed against the finding, won his appeal and was acquitted during a fresh trial.

The story illustrates, among other things, the powerful effect that our non-verbal behaviour can have and the interpretations others make.

Body language

Non-verbal behaviour is frequently referred to as 'body language'.

Just as in the murder trial story, when you communicate with other people, it's not *what* you say but the *way* you say it. You communicate not only with words but also with your emotions, feelings and intentions. These manifest themselves through your non-verbal behaviour or body language.

Body language relates to such elements as posture, distance/space, gestures, facial expressions, head movement and eye contact.

Non-verbal aspects of speech include volume, tone, pitch, voice quality, speed of speaking, pausing, accent and emphasis (see **Figure 4.1**).

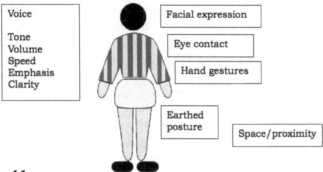

Figure 4.1

Albert Mehrabian's research (1967) provides the basis for the widely quoted and often much over-simplified statistic for the effectiveness of spoken communication. Mehrabian did not intend the statistic to be used or applied freely to all communications and meaning, but to communications of feelings and attitudes.

In this context, he found:
7% of meaning is in the words that are spoken
38% of meaning is in the way that the words are said
55% of meaning is in facial expression.

Invariably, the *real* message, what we really mean, is not contained in the words but conveyed through our non-verbal behaviour. This is because our words say one thing and our body language another. If there is a dilemma you choose, most times, to believe the non-verbal behaviour.

Congruence

When there is a disparity between *what* you say and *how* you say it, people are more likely to be convinced by *how* you say it. When you are congruent your non-verbal behaviour matches what you are saying. When someone says "I love you", the words alone are not enough. Indeed, there are times in our lives when this has been said and not believed at all! These non-verbal behaviours act as the *carriers of the truth.*

In conversation we can be so focused on what we are saying that we are oblivious to the many non-verbal messages we are sending out. You may think you can disguise your attitude by consciously choosing or fixing your words but your body language betrays what is really going on. It is far more difficult to fix the unconscious messages conveyed by numerous bits of body language.

Sometimes it is obvious that there is a mismatch between your intentions and your behaviour. We know it and so do other people. Other times you can walk away from a conversation thinking you have achieved what you want only to find out later the other person has interpreted your message very differently.

Paying attention to, but not being obsessed by your body language can help you understand why you sometimes create this lack of congruence. You can find out how you're being perceived in a number of ways.

You may be fortunate to have a friend, partner or really trustworthy colleague who gives you honest and useful feedback in a way that makes it easy for you to accept and adjust. Or you may have been in situations where the feedback is given more crudely and with some degree of angst.

Or you can choose to become more aware of the effects of your body language by completing the following exercises in this chapter.

Our mind is like a parachute – it works best when it is open. This also seems true of our body language. You can take the concept of 'open' to your:
- stance and posture
- facial expression
- hand gestures and movement.

Exercise 4.1: ADOPTING AN EARTHED POSITION

A very practical way of getting body and mind into an open posture is something we call the earthed position. The impression the earthed position gives is one of strength and confidence. Not only is it an impression, in the earthed position, you will feel more resourceful, strong and adaptable.

To stand in an earthed position:
- plant both feet firmly on the ground
- relax into your body
- open yourself up wide and let go of any tension in your body from your shoulders downwards
- open the palms of your hands.

The earthed position can equally help you when you are seated:
- plant your feet firmly on the floor
- support your back with the back of the chair – you will notice that by sitting like this your back becomes straighter and your upper body more open and your head alert and more erect
- open the palms of your hands and rest your hands on your lap.

Body and mind

The reason you feel this strength from within is because 'body and mind' are irrevocably linked to each other, dovetailing as a part of the same system. What happens to one part of the system influences the other.

When you accept mind and body as one system you can use this understanding as a tool to change your thinking and your feelings. You can experience this by doing the following exercise.

Exercise 4.2: CHANGING THE WAY . . .

I'd like you to think of a situation that would make you very angry.

For the purpose of the exercise, allow yourself angry thoughts about something or someone.

As you hold on to these feelings or thoughts imagine speaking to that person and adopt an 'earthed' position:

- your face open and relaxed
- your chest and upper body wide and open
- keep any gestures relaxed and open
- keep the palms of your hands open
- speak in a slow measured way
- breath slowly and deeply.

If you have managed to keep yourself 'open' as you were doing this exercise I imagine you have been unable to maintain any real level of anger.

You can't do all of the above and maintain your anger because your mind says, *"To be **congruent**, when I'm angry my body shows a set of responses I'm now not showing – I cannot have angry thoughts and open body language – one or other has to change!"*

This **body and mind** arrangement gives you an opportunity to change your mental state either by changing your thoughts or changing your body language. You can't always choose the situations you find yourself in, but you can choose the way in which you want to behave.

Use this technique next time you're facing a situation where you want to remain assertive and don't have time to get your thoughts in order, e.g. as in the case of handling aggression.

On the telephone

We have discussed how your body language plays a significant part in your face-to-face interactions with others, but how much effect does it have when the other person cannot see you, as in a telephone conversation? We've all had the experience of speaking with someone on the phone for a number of years but may have never met them. You will have formed an image in your own mind of what they look like and what kind of person they are. When you eventually get to see them in the flesh, it can be a big surprise!

Anyone who has received Customer Care training and has been asked to smile on the telephone will tell you smiling makes a huge difference to how you are perceived. Smiling causes the other elements of your voice to change. You can warm your hands in the afterglow of a warm smile and what a difference it makes!

Although people cannot see your body language over the phone they do experience the effects of how you are standing, sitting or slouching; where you have your attention, whether you are being distracted by what is going on or whether you are focused on them.

Your voice and all its variations obviously play a significant part of the impression. The elements of body language associated with the voice are volume, tone, pitch, speed, clarity, pausing, accent, emphasis and the use of silence (see **Figure 4.1**, page 19).

The exercise below gives you an opportunity to practise changing the impact you have on the telephone by changing your voice. You can get good feedback if you enlist the help of a friend, colleague or partner and convince them to try the exercise as well!

Exercise 4.3: ADJUST THE VOICE TO CHANGE THE IMPACT

"I want you to replace this design with another one that looks more professional."

Repeat the sentence above to practise the different impacts you can have by adjusting the:

speed and pace – experiment with slow, fast or measured

volume – try soft, loud or moderate

tone – experiment with deep, high pitched or monotone

endings – end your sentence in a high pitch and then try ending with a much lower tone

change the emphasis on certain words – "I", "need", "you"

pause – in different places.

We would recommend that the tougher the situation you have to deal with, the more you make that telephone call from an earthed position.

People on our courses often ask if changing 'bits' of body language means changing their personality. Changing body language does not change your personality, though in the grand scheme of things it will have positive effects on how you are perceived. That, in turn, will affect your sense of self. And, in that way, you may see yourself very differently.

Reference
Mehrabian, A. and Ferris, S. (1967) Inference of attitudes from nonverbal communication in two channels. *Journal of Consulting Psychology*, 31(3): 248–52.

CHAPTER 5

VISUALISATION

Being clear about what you want

As we said earlier, when you are really clear about what you want and when you want it – you are much more likely to get it!

Some years ago we lived in Kent in a 16th century farmhouse. We inherited from the previous owner a number of garden ornaments including an original farmyard cart, the type a 19th century farmer would have used to transport goods to and from market. Painted in pastel colours it helped to create a picture of rural bliss positioned at the entrance to the property.

Sadly, after a couple of years the cart looked worse for wear. It had taken a beating from small children, dogs and general bouts of harsh weather. So, one Sunday, when we were gardening we decided that it would be great if we could just conjure up a replacement. We realised that this wouldn't be an easy task and indeed if we did find one we'd have the difficulty and expense of transporting it and then making it blend into the surroundings like the last one. We felt a real affinity to this piece of historic transport that we'd inherited and wanted to do the best we could to keep its memory alive and the ambience it created. So we did a sketch of the cart, took some photos and went about writing an advert to go into the 'wanted' section of our local paper. We promised ourselves to do the best we could to find a replacement.

The next day we were visiting a customer close to Heathrow airport, a decidedly urban area with some residential development. As we drove out of their car park, directly opposite was a commercial storage depot with several warehouses and a modern bungalow adjacent. A number of removal vans were parked in the driveway of the bungalow and in the garden was an *exact* replica of our farmyard cart! It really couldn't have been more out of place if it had tried.

We jumped out of the car and knocked on the door: no reply, so we left a note and our business card asking if they would be interested in selling. That evening we received a call from the owner who was keen to sell the cart and offered to transport it to Kent the next day in one of his removal vans as one of his lads was doing a job not far from us.

Visualisation is a mental technique that uses the power of your senses to create an outcome or a result you want. To have a full sensory picture of the end in mind helps to make your dreams come true. Begin with the end in mind.

You and I can constantly be in a dream state. Indeed, some psychologists believe that most of us dream away our lives because few are able to stay in the here and now. We are either remembering or living in the past or worrying and being concerned about the future.

Our internal thoughts and chats with ourselves (see Chapter 6 Self-talk) materially affect and shape how we move into the future. Creation happens twice: once in your mind and then in reality.

Visualisation is a personal vision and a mental rehearsal for success – a way to provide us with the mental resources and determination to help us succeed.

How do you do visualisation?

You have five senses that help you make meaning and sense of the world. The five senses are seeing, hearing, feeling, smell and taste. You use all these senses but may have a preference for a particular sense above another – one you trust more than others. You may certainly be aware of how much you and those closest to you rely on the main three senses.

Do you know people who seem to forget anything you tell them unless they actually *see* it written down? Just telling them something doesn't do it for them! They prefer to communicate through their sense of sight. They will be endlessly drawing pictures and diagrams to illustrate their point of view.

Others want to read about it, *hear* the tape and speak with people before they can properly absorb the information.

Still others, on the other hand, fail to absorb and remember anything unless they *feel* it, touch it and experience it. No amount of telling or showing will do.

There is no one way for everyone. Different people do it differently, using their preferred and trusted sense.

In terms of accomplishing anything, your mind is neutral; the only thing it asks of you is *that* you choose. When it knows what you want it can marshal resources, mental and physical, to achieve it.

Visualisation doesn't guarantee success but it does significantly increase the chances. The more you can make a full sensual representation of the future, the more enticing and compelling it will be for you to succeed. Use as many of your senses as you can to create a picture, a movie, a story of the outcome you want.

As you start the visualisation process, do so on the basis that this future is an example of your success. This will normally represent a win:win (see pages 65 and 66 to see how you create win:win).

Beware – if you were to choose a disaster as your future creation, chances are it will become self-fulfilling. Remember – your mind does not care which outcome you choose, only that you choose one.

The questions you need to ask yourself at the start of the visualisation process are associated with the main sensory categories of seeing, hearing and feeling.

On some occasions, adding the senses of *taste* and *smell* would give you an even clearer picture of the future and in some instances these two senses would be very important to include in the future picture:

- ***What are you seeing?***
- ***What are you hearing?***
- ***What are you feeling?***

Note – although you go into the future to create your visualisation, describe your thoughts in the *present* tense, e.g. imagine it is happening *now*.

What are you seeing (in the future)?

Take a moment to think of a situation in the future where you want to be successful. Write down and/or draw the answers to the questions below:

When you visualise the situation in your mind, what do you see?

Where are you, in a room, at home, in your office, in the corridor, etc.?

Is the environment dark or light? Play with the brightness inside your mind to find a lightness that becomes empowering – too bright may be too strong, too dark too energy sapping.

Who is there with you?

Where are they, what are they doing?

How do you now see yourself? What is your posture like? What gestures are you making? Are you sitting or standing? How is your facial expression, open or closed, rigid or free from tension? Are you smiling? How much eye contact are you giving and to whom?

How does the other person(s) look when you are how you want to be? What is their face like, etc.?

How are they regarding you now? Are you giving both them and yourself respect?

What are you hearing (in the future)?
When you imagine the situation, what do you hear?

How is your voice sounding? Do you hear yourself using certain words or phrases?

How are you emphasising your words, etc.?

How fast or slow are you talking?

How loud or soft is your voice?

How are you pausing and allowing yourself time to give the best reply? Are you allowing gaps and how are you using the gift of silence? What kind of phrases are you using?

What kind of questions are you asking?

What kind of things does the other person say to you?

How is the other person(s) replying now you are giving both them and yourself respect?

What are the things they are saying and how are they saying them, etc.?

What are you feeling (in the future)?
Describe the feelings you have and then give them some texture, e.g. I *feel* excited.

Where in your body is each feeling located?

What kind of a feeling is it? For example, "It's a tingling feeling and it's like a warm glow, it starts in my diaphragm and fills my head." *(No! You are not going daft – trust me!)*

How do I want others to feel?

The more times and situations you can visualise your success, the more you will find you are achieving what you want.

Exercise 5.1: IT'S ALL IN THE MIND (PART 1)

Here is an exercise you might like to do to find out how good you are at visualising. To find out what kind of an imager you are, complete the following questionnaire. Before you start, close your eyes, and take a few deep breaths. Then open your eyes and read the first question.

This is not a timed exercise.

When the image has become as clear as you can make it, open your eyes and write down a rating, in accordance with the following scale.

■ Fairly clear	2
■ Vague but recognisable	1
■ Little or no image	0

1. Seeing
Visualise the following: **Rating**

a.   a candle flame   ....
b.   a red sunset   ....
c.   swans flying   ....
d.   a hand writing a note on white paper   ....
e.   a red triangle on green paper   ....
f.   a three-digit number, written on a wall   ....
g.   an endless desert   ....
h.   waves breaking on a beach   ....
i.   yourself getting into a car   ....
j.   the outside of the building you live in   ....
                                              Score   ....

2. Hearing
Imagine the following sounds:

a.   a deep gong reverberating   ....

b.   a telephone ringing   ....
c.   a voice calling your name   ....
d.   the noise of traffic   ....
e.   children playing   ....
f.   a pigeon cooing   ....
g.   a jet plane passing overhead   ....
h.   a stone falling into a lake   ....
i.   voices in the next room   ....
j.   a favourite piece of music   ....
       Score   ....

3. Feeling
Imagine what it feels like to be:
a.   chopping wood energetically   ....
b.   running slowly along a wet beach   ....
c.   swimming in the sea   ....
d.   playing a ball game   ....
e.   driving a car   ....
       Score   ....

Imagine the feeling of touching:
a.   sandpaper   ....
b.   silk   ....
c.   an orange   ....
d.   a cat   ....
e.   someone's hand   ....
       Score   ....

Now add up the scores **Total score**   ....

If you have scored 50 or more, you already have the ability to create strong visual representations and will be able to use this skill straightaway.

If you scored between 26 and 49, you have a reasonably good visualising ability and will be able to make use of it in many areas. You will need, however, to practise.

If you scored 25 or less, you will be unlikely to find visualising easy at the moment. You can develop the skills with regular practice over a period of weeks.

Exercise 5.2: IT'S ALL IN THE MIND (PART 2)

Think of a situation you're going to face in the future, one that you anticipate may be tough or one perhaps you haven't managed as well as you would have liked in the past and it's likely to re-occur.

First of all, relax and get in touch with your breathing, notice your in-breath . . . and your out-breath. Do this several times and, as you do so, you will probably notice that your breathing goes deeper and slower.

As you observe your breathing, fast forward to your future situation and see yourself being successful.

You are achieving the result you want, which is good for you and also good for the other person. Now enter this future situation and ask yourself the see, hear and feel questions.

See

Where are you, in a room, at home, in your office, in the corridor, etc.?

Is the environment dark or light? Play with the brightness inside your mind to find a lightness that becomes empowering – too bright may be too strong, too dark too energy sapping.

Who is there with you?

Where are they, what are they doing?

How do you want to see yourself? What would you like your posture to be? What gestures are you making? Are you sitting or standing? How is your facial expression, open or closed, rigid or free from tension? Are you smiling? How much eye contact are you giving and to whom?

How does the other person(s) look when you are how you want

to be? What is their face like, etc.?
How are they regarding you now you are giving both them and
yourself respect?

Hear

How is your voice sounding? Do you hear yourself using certain
words or phrases?
How are you emphasising your words, etc.?
How fast or slow are you talking?
How loud or soft is your voice?
How are you pausing and allowing yourself time to give the best
reply? Are you allowing gaps and how are you using the gift of
silence?
What kind of phrases are you using?
What kind of questions are you asking?
What kind of things does the other person say to you?
How is the other person(s) replying now you are giving both them
and yourself respect?
What are the things they are saying and how are they saying them,
etc.?

Feel

Describe the feelings you have.
Where in your body is each feeling located?
What kind of a feeling is it?
How do you want others to feel?

You may now view this future situation completely differently with
a great deal more enthusiasm, energy and confidence in your
ability to get the result you have envisaged.

You have taken the first steps in making it become true for you.

CHAPTER 6
SELF-TALK

The mini tape recorders were strapped to Ben and Caroline's wrists. Both young children were part of a research group: the entire project involved several hundred children.

At the end of each day the tape was removed and a fresh one inserted. At the end of the week the tapes were collected and all the conversations were analysed and categorised.

A total of 95% of what was said to the kids turned out to be *negative* in some way or another.

If this legacy is representative of a larger public, you and me, it's a wonder that so many of us turn out to be essentially OK. We all, however, have ghosts in the machine, struggle and are blighted by old tape recordings and videos embedded deeply in our psyche that we play endlessly inside our heads.

If I asked you the question, "Who do you talk to most during your normal day?", you might be tempted to answer: your spouse/partner, your children, specific work colleagues or friends, your mum and dad, etc.

The answer, of course, is none of these. The answer is *you!*

The things we say to ourselves

If you are influenced by what other people say to you, imagine how much more are you influenced by what you *say* to yourself?

You spend your day talking to *yourself* inside your head. You remember conversations or past events: you conjure up dialogue or future situations. You then continuously discuss with yourself how you'll behave and how these situations will turn out. If you've had a bad experience, or in some way let yourself down, you replay the 'tape' in an endless loop, amplifying your every mistake and mishap.

Your *inner thoughts* play a significant part in establishing how you *feel*, which in turn determines how you *act* (see **Figure 6.1**).

What you THINK leads to how you FEEL
What you FEEL leads to how you BEHAVE

Figure 6.1

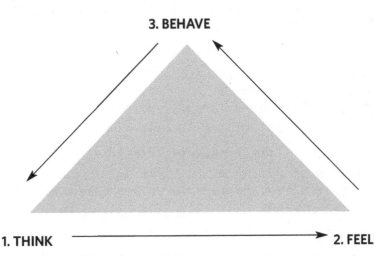

For most of us, these *inner conversations* or *self-talk* are verbal exchanges inside our head. For others, it is less of a conversation and more of a picture or a movie completely uncensored, the director's cut.

However, these tapes or movies are going on in the background like mood music, shaping your expectations, setting the atmosphere with your unconscious mind in charge. When you do become aware of something happening inside, it is often your feelings that alert you to the fact that *something isn't quite right*. However, these feelings are brought about by your thinking process.

Certain sounds, sights and places can act as anchors and have the most enlivening and /or unsettling affects. These experiences – *real* or *imaginary* – are *stored* or *anchored* deep in our *subconscious*.

This causal model of behaviour (**Figure 6.1**) shows the chain reaction that starts with thinking and results in behaving.

If I am *confident* and *assured* in handling a situation it is because I *feel* good about myself and I *think* I can succeed. If, on the other hand, I *behave* defensively and nervously it is because I am *feeling* threatened and can't cope because I *think* the other person is too strong and I am too weak.

When the results you are getting are not what you want, you are not destined to repeat history. You can intervene at the *thinking* stage or the *feeling* stage and thus change what you do and the result.

Disempowering self-talk

In **Figure 6.2** we demonstrate how disempowering self-talk can lead to negative feelings, which would lead to being aggressive or, more likely, non-assertive.

Situation

You're standing in for your manager at the monthly review meeting. There will be three directors and several senior managers present and you know that a couple of them can be quite aggressive.

You consider what the meeting might be like for you – see **Figure 6.2**.

With such mixed **negative feelings,** the knock-on effect on behaviour is that this individual has *talked themselves into a mindset* where it is unlikely they will succeed in favourably representing themself or their department.

If you could be a fly on the wall what might you observe at the meeting?

Figure 6.2

Disempowering self-talk	Negative feelings
Leads to "There will be lots of important people all around me; if anyone asks what I'm doing it'll be so embarrassing."	Leads to Embarrassment and fear of blushing
"I must sit still and not look nervous or fidget."	Nervousness and fear
"It will be easier if I just accept that I'm not in their league, keep my head down so I don't bring attention to myself."	Inadequacy
"I'll stutter and stumble when I talk. Last time I tried to handle Giles's aggressive remarks I got nowhere; it'll be the same this time."	Hopeless inevitability
"All senior people are so full of their own importance; I never know what to say."	Self-deprecation
"Well, if they start on about delays to the programme, I'll just remind them that they're the ones who asked for the impossible!"	Anger and resentment
"I won't be able to get them interested in how the staff feel about the changes; I'll be a singe voice in the wilderness."	Weakness and isolation

Results in
Hesitancy – stuttering – mumbling – speaking softly without self-belief – easily put off – resigned to not getting respect – angry with both themselves and the senior management team – *"I'll never be asked to deputise again!"*

The nature of disempowering self-talk

Pessimistic view of the future
"There will be lots of important people all around me; if anyone asks what I'm doing there, it'll be so embarrassing."

Absolute thinking
"I'll stutter and stumble when I talk."
"Last time I tried to handle Giles's aggressive remarks I got nowhere; it'll be the same this time."

Exaggerating
"All senior people are so full of their own importance; I never know what to say."

Assumptions
"I won't be able to get them interested in how the staff feel about the changes."

Unbalanced view
"I'll be a singe voice in the wilderness."

Empowering self-talk

You are not a prisoner of your own unconscious negative thoughts. The first thing you need to do to regain control is to bring the negative thoughts to your conscious attention. You need to slow down your thinking and look at what you are visualising or saying to yourself. You will be amazed when you ask yourself, *"What am I saying to myself?"* Or, if your thoughts are represented visually, *"What am I seeing happening?"*

Ask yourself these questions and listen to the answer. Many people find it helpful to write down what they are thinking so they can slow their thoughts and examine them dispassionately. Once you challenge the veracity of what you've written you will be able to start the process of making new choices.

Figure 6.3 Reframing Self Talk

Disempowering self-talk	Empowering self-talk
"There will be lots of important people all around me; if anyone asks what I'm doing there it'll be so embarrassing."	"I know information that senior people don't; that's why they've asked me to be there."
"I must sit still and not look nervous or fidget."	"I can be relaxed and sit back in my chair and show that I'm listening."
"It will be easier if I just accept that I'm not in their league, keep my head down so I don't bring attention to myself."	"I'm there for a good reason. I have spoken calmly and clearly many times before in meetings."
"I'll stutter and stumble when I talk. Last time I tried to handle Giles's aggressive remarks I got nowhere: it'll be the same this time."	"I can trust myself to say the right thing; I can be firm and direct with Giles and stay committed to what I believe."
"All senior people are so full of their own importance; I never know what to say."	"Most of the managers are not there to score points but to sort out the issues. I can contribute when I think it's appropriate."
"Well, if they start on about delays to the programme, I'll just remind them that they're the ones who asked for the impossible!"	"They have a right to question and challenge how far we've progressed with the programme. I can give them my view."
"I won't be able to get them interested in how the staff feel about the changes, I'll be a singe voice in the wilderness."	"They have listened in the past and I can explain how the concerns of the staff are affecting the programme."

You can choose, as in **Figure 6.3,** to replace any **disempowering self-talk** with much more **empowering self-talk.**

With a different, more realistic set of thoughts and feelings, this individual has a greater chance of resolving the situation in a satisfactory way.

The nature of empowering self-talk

Realistic view of the future

"I can be relaxed and sit back in my chair and show that I'm listening."
"I can wait for the appropriate moment and stay calm and collected."

Objective

"They have a right to question and challenge how far we've progressed with the programme. I can give them my view."

Noticing the positive

"I know information that senior people don't; that's why they've asked me to be there."

Honest about the past

"They have listened in the past and I can explain how the concerns of the staff are effecting the programme."

Can-do approach

"I can trust myself to say the right thing; I can be firm and direct with Giles and stay committed to what I believe."

When you are being successful and achieving what you want, you don't need to check the things you say to yourself – whatever is happening is clearly working.

For those times, however, when you feel:
- under pressure
- threatened
- lacking your normal self-confidence

■ you're facing disaster and it is not going to work out well for you, it's time to reach out for some extra help from within. Try this technique out now.

Exercise 6.1: SELF-TALK – PREPARING FOR A FUTURE SITUATION

This exercise will give you practice at developing your skill in replacing disempowering self-talk with empowering self-talk.

Choose a situation you're facing at work that might be causing you some concern.

1. Ask yourself, "*What am I saying to myself?*"

2. Write down what you're saying in the left-hand column below.

3. Highlight any of the **pessimistic, exaggerated, unbalanced views, etc.**

4. Adjust them, and write a more realistic, objective, positive and honest version in the right-hand column.

Disempowering self-talk	Empowering self-talk

You will find this a very helpful tool to use before you face difficult situations and the more you use it, the less you will have to write things down.

When you look at your **empowering self-talk** a couple of phrases may leap out at you as being significant in keeping you on track. Write them down separately or highlight them and use them as a 'mantra' that you can chant to yourself before and during the situation.

Soon you will find you can do it in 'real time' and you only need to create a space with a pause or a moment of silence to consider what you are saying to yourself.

Intervening at the *feeling* level

The second way of intervening in the **THINK – FEEL – BEHAVE** triangle (**Figure 6.1**) is at the *feeling* level.

When thinking about a future situation you need to ask yourself,

"How do I want to feel in this situation?" and write down the feelings, e.g. *prepared, calm, confident*; two or three important feelings are enough.

Then write down what you need to say to yourself to bring about those feelings and check that these thoughts are **empowering**.

Check once more that this **empowering self-talk** does deliver the feelings you want. If not, ask yourself, *"Which thoughts will deliver these feelings?"* and write them down. Carry on until you are satisfied that what you're saying will deliver the feelings you want.

Make the significant parts a 'mantra' and repeat them out loud in your head just before you go into the situation.

Both type of interventions work – enjoy the experience!

CHAPTER 7

RIGHTS AND PERSONAL PERMISSION

Many of the ideas now associated with assertiveness training were first proposed in Manuel J. Smith's book, *When I Say No, I Feel Guilty*, published in 1975. The book explains that assertiveness is largely about expressing oneself clearly and resisting manipulation. It proclaims a '**Bill of Assertive Rights**'.

'Bill of Assertive Rights'

You have the right to judge your own behaviour, thoughts and emotions, and to take the responsibility for their initiation and consequences upon yourself.

You have the right to offer no reasons or excuses for justifying your behaviour.

You have the right to judge if you are responsible for finding solutions to other people's problems.

You have the right to change your mind.

You have the right to make mistakes – and be responsible for them.

You have the right to say, "*I don't know*".

You have the right to be independent of the goodwill of others before coping with them.

You have the right to be illogical in making decisions.

You have the right to say, *"I don't understand"*.

You have the right to say, *"I don't care"*.

Giving yourself permission

No doubt there have been times in your life when you've been uncertain about whether what you want to do is 'right'. You may well have had conversations with yourself that asked, *"Have I the right to say this? Do I have **permission** to do this? Am I justified in asking for this?"*

Equally, at times you may have thought, *"This person has no right to do that or treat me in this way!"* This thinking can prevent you behaving assertively in situations where you/others actually *do* have the right.

'Rights' are central to behaving assertively.

A right is something to which you are justly entitled.

Rights are the key to living your life in a balanced and assertive way.

When you act upon these rights but do not give the same rights to others, your behaviour becomes aggressive. When you give others rights that you do not also claim for yourself, your behaviour becomes submissive or non-assertive. When you accept rights for yourself and also give them to others, your behaviour is likely to be in balance, assertive and in the spirit of win:win. The balancing of rights provides internal **permission** and affirmation to behave in an assertive way.

Rights and responsibilities

Rights are like picking up a stick. When you pick up a stick you pick up both ends. Similarly, when you pick up a *Right* you also pick up a *Responsibility*. For instance, if you claim the right to be *human and make mistakes* you need to accept the **responsibilities** that are attached to it:

■ to have taken due care
■ to admit your mistake
■ to learn from the mistake
■ not repeat the same mistake again
■ to ask for help if you don't know how to correct it.

Otherwise, acting on rights would be an open cheque book for avoiding responsibility and the consequences of your behaviour.

Sometimes you may act on your rights out of frustration, anger or as the last resort. If so, you may remember your self-talk and the tone of that internal voice: *"Right, that's it, I have a **right** to do this!"* The likelihood is that you acted aggressively and got the balance wrong.

Particularly, when you are faced with difficult situations or where you are unsure what to do, thinking through your and others' rights will lead you to behaving assertively. In Exercise 7.1 below are some general rights that apply in a range of situations. It is important to know:

■ which are the rights you currently accept for yourself *and act upon*?
■ which are the rights you give to others and allow them to *act upon*?
■ doing the exercise may give you an indication of how assertive you are and in what areas you need to further develop.

Exercise 7.1: MY RIGHTS AND OTHERS' RIGHTS

First, tick the **rights** you 'give yourself' in the left-hand column, then tick the **rights** you 'give others' in the right-hand column.

Warning: Be aware you may be drawn to do this exercise from an intellectual perspective. At a rational level, the rights make fundamental sense and intellectually it's easy to tick both left and right columns. However, rights become real only when you act upon them.

Tick the ones you 'give yourself'	Commonly held rights	Tick the ones you 'give others'
	I have the right to say yes or no, without feeling guilty.	
	I have the right to state my own needs and set my own priorities.	
	I have the right to be treated with respect as an intelligent, capable and equal human being.	
	I have the right to have and express my own feelings and opinions, even if they are different from those of others.	
	I have the right to be listened to and taken seriously.	
	I have the right to make mistakes and be responsible for them.	
	I have the right to change my mind without making excuses.	
	I have the right to say, "I don't understand".	
	I have the right to say, "I don't know".	
	I have the right to ask for what I want.	

Tick the ones you 'give yourself'	Commonly held rights	Tick the ones you 'give others'
	I have the right to decline responsibility for other people's problems.	
	I have the right to deal with others without being dependent on them for approval.	
	I have the right to ask for information.	
	I have the right not to satisfy some people some times.	
	I have the right to sometimes do less than the maximum which is humanly possible.	
	I have the right to think before I answer.	
	I have the right to present myself to the world as I am, without making excuses.	
	I have the right to be treated with respect.	
	I have the right to have others respect my rights.	
	I have the right to ask for support from others.	

You'll find greater benefit from the exercise if you ask yourself, *"Is this true for me in every situation, or are there specific times when I don't act as if these were my rights, or when I don't give them to others?"*

From an assertive perspective, the 'ideal' scenario would be that for every tick you've put in the left-hand column you've also put one in the right. If you don't have this distribution, congratulations, you're not perfect – join the human race!

If you have more ticks in the left column than the right, there are likely to be parts of your behaviour that are aggressive. On the other hand, if you have more ticks on the right, you are likely to be passive and non-assertive in many situations.

When you reflect on past situations that haven't worked out the way you wanted, you'll probably find that this exercise provides you with clues as to why they didn't. Equally, when everything went as you wanted, your rights would have been nicely balanced.

Rights are one of the fundamental building blocks of your personal power base. Remember, nobody can take your dignity or your rights away unless you give them away.

CHAPTER 8
BELIEFS

We looked at the effect of self-talk and rights on your behaviour, but where do some of these messages and ideas that pop up in our self-talk come from?

Why do we hold on to these ideas and thoughts despite being faced with evidence to the contrary that they don't work or are unhelpful to us? Frequently, people come on our programmes having been asked to change and yet will say, "I can't do that; it's just not me" or "I could never do that; it's not what I believe" or "I'm too old to change".

No matter how many techniques and 'tricks of the trade' they're presented with, if they don't fit in to who they think they are, it will always feel alien to them.

What you have deep down inside you is a set of beliefs that guide your behaviour and shape who you are. Beliefs are the assumptions we make about ourselves, about others, the world in general and how we expect things to be. They are a conviction and acceptance that certain things are true or real without the necessary supporting evidence.

We usually think of beliefs in terms of creeds or doctrines, and many beliefs are. But in the most basic sense, a belief is any *guiding principle, dictum, or view that can provide meaning and direction in life.*

Beliefs guide us in many ways:

- They act as filters to our perception of the world; we see, hear and feel what we want to see, hear and feel. It's our reality and perhaps no one else's.
- They either empower us, or limit our behaviour. Many of these limitations are self-imposed.

■ They are invisible, but manifest themselves through the actions we take.

They become self-fulfilling prophecies – *'Argue for your limitations and you have them.'*

Types of beliefs

Beliefs can be about you, about situations or other people. For example, you may have beliefs about *who you are* that take the form:

■ "I am . . .
■ clever
■ clumsy
■ successful
■ lazy
■ attractive."

Or you may have beliefs about other people:

■ "Never trust a sales person."
■ "Politicians are all the same."
■ "People are only concerned with No.1."

Or about situations and life in general:

■ "Loyalty is a thing of the past."
■ "Unless you shout no one hears you."
■ "Showing vulnerability is a sign of weakness."

There are beliefs that *prevent* you from doing things – phrases that begin with:

■ "I can't . . . I mustn't . . .
■ . . . show my feelings
■ . . . let people down
■ . . . tell others what I really want."

There are beliefs that *compel* us or *oblige* us to do things – phrases that begin with:

■ "I must . . . I should . . .

■ ... get this absolutely perfect
■ ... give as good as I get
■ ... show them how clever I am."

Where do our beliefs come from?

We sometimes tell a story on our programmes that resonate with people about how beliefs are formed.

A young couple, Sally and Martin, got married.

One night when they were on their honeymoon on some sun-drenched island sipping their 'sundowners' and watching the big orange ball sink slowly below the horizon, they turned to each other and began musing about their wedding day. How their parents had in every way 'pushed the boat out' to give them the perfect day.

They then began thinking of their eventual return home and how they were going to repay the generosity of their parents.

They decided to invite their mums and dads to the inaugural meal they would cook as newly weds.

The afternoon of the great day arrived and Sally and Martin busied themselves preparing the lunch.

At an early stage in the preparations Martin noticed that Sally took out the very large joint of meat and cut off roughly a third, put it away in the fridge and placed the other two-thirds in the oven. Martin was curious why Sally did this, but knowing Sally, believed she had good reason for doing this.

The lunch was a great success and they were showered with compliments over the cooking. Spurred on by their success, Sally and Martin decided to widen the net and invite the grandparents as well next time.

The day arrived and they were both again in the kitchen preparing the food. Martin watched again as Sally took the joint of meat, cut off roughly a third and placed two-thirds in the oven. Given that they were cooking for more people than before, Martin was curious and asked Sally why she had done this. Sally's reply was that she had learned this approach from her mother and had always done it this way.

Still curious he left the kitchen and went to ask Sally's mum why she did this. Her reply was that she had learned to cook from her mum and had always done it that way.

Fortunately Sally's grandma was also there and Martin turned to her with the same question. Her reply was . . .

"When Grandad and I first got married we lived in a poky little flat that had the bare necessities and a very small cooker. Whatever size of joint we bought we always had to chop a piece off or it wouldn't fit – and from then on it just become a habit." A habit that she continued even when she moved to a more spacious home.

Many of our beliefs are formed at an early age between the ages of 0–7 years. The 'child' within us will have taken on board unreservedly many of the things we now hold deeply as truths.

We will have adopted sayings and dictums from 'big' people in our lives because we love and respect them, have learned to trust what they say and believe in what they say. By 'big' people we mean parents, grandparents, teachers, older siblings, etc.

We are equally influenced by the society and culture in which we live, we grow to accept and value certain things and devalue others.

We may experience traumatic events in our lives and, in the moments of shock, import other people's strong views and opinions and not question them.

A course member told us of a traumatic event in her life when she was 'stood up' at the altar, waiting for a bridegroom who never turned up. In that moment someone whispered in her ear a barrage of expletives and the dictum, "Typical: you can never trust men!" This she believed from then on, and it blighted her life and relationships for a very long time (her words not ours).

Enabling or unhelpful beliefs

Some beliefs restrict and limit your growth, keep you fearful and insecure, encourage you to think you are not worthy of love and respect. They seduce you into feeling powerless and ineffective.

Other beliefs help you grow, expand your horizons and build your confidence. Holding them helps you believe you can make a positive impact on your world, and support you in your desire to be happy and healthy.

Exercise 8.1: ENABLING OR UNHELPFUL BELIEFS?

A few commonly held work-based beliefs are given below.

First decide whether you think the belief is one that enables you and helps you, 'E', or one that would limit or restrict you and be unhelpful in some way or other, 'U'.

>   Place your **E** or **U** in the first box.

Then tick the right-hand box if this belief is true for you, e.g. you currently hold it.

U / E

Example: My needs are more important than others ☑ ☐

In this example the person has decided that this is an example of an unhelpful belief and also thinks that it is true for them.

You can check your answers against our views below.

U / E

1. Others are more important, more powerful and in some way better than me. ☐ ☐

2. I am free to make my own decisions in life. ☐ ☐

3. If you want a job done well, do it yourself. ☐ ☐

4. My opinion is generally not valued. ☐ ☐

5. Challenging a senior manager's view is a
limiting career move. ☐ ☐

6. A refusal is an attack on me personally. ☐ ☐

7. Other people can't be trusted. ☐ ☐

8. You get what you deserve in life. ☐ ☐

9. If I ask people to do things, they'll think
I am rude or bossy. ☐ ☐

10. I do not need permission to take action. ☐ ☐

11. Manners make the man. ☐ ☐

12 In life, you have to give as good as you get. ☐ ☐

13. Avoid conflict at all costs. ☐ ☐

14. Be strong at all times and never show
your weaknesses. ☐ ☐

15. In order to be liked I have to be what others
want me to be. ☐ ☐

16. A leopard can't change his spots. ☐ ☐

17. Only I can give away my dignity and self-respect. ☐ ☐

Suggested answers:

1. An **unhelpful non-assertive** belief. Leads to putting others first,
not pursuing your own needs with any vigour and commitment.

2. An **enabling assertive** belief. You are free to make your own

decisions, be reponsible for yourself and create your own destiny. You also need to recognise you have to live with the consequences.

3. Generally an **unhelpful** belief. It is entirely appropriate on occasions that you need to tell people things in order to get things done. But to do so excessively leads to the same effect as No 1. If you treat people like monkeys, monkeys is what you'll get!

4. An **unhelpful non-assertive** belief. You have a right to express your view or opinion. It doesn't mean it is true, but it is as valid as anyone else's. Holding an unassertive belief like this will lead to low self-esteem, a loss of respect from others.

5. An **unhelpful non-assertive** belief. Your contribution is valid and if you have an idea or solution worth putting forward, then you have the responsibility to share it with others to enable good decision-making.

It is OK to disagree with others – how you do it becomes very important. Persisting with the belief can lead to a world of 'Yes minister' and imperfect solutions.

6. An **unhelpful aggressive** belief. In the same way you have a right to your views and opinions, to challenge and to express doubt or concern, so do others. Holding this belief can lead you to becoming defensive, withdrawing from situations or attacking those who have a contrary view to your own.

7. An **unhelpful aggressive** belief. Holding this belief leads to lack of trust, poor-quality relationships, overwork and resentment. It will often accompany a stressful lifestyle, leading to health problems as you try to fix everything and find there are not enough hours in the day.

8. An **unhelpful non-assertive** belief. The assumption behind this belief is that there is a greater power (fate) outside of your own

control that determines whether you are deserving or not. Holding this belief can lead to apathy and resignation and remove responsibility.

9. An **unhelpful non-assertive** belief. Holding this belief can prevent you asking for help and, as a manager, stops you delegating. You end up doing someone else's work. As with most things, it's not what you say, but how you say it.

10. An **enabling assertive belief**. There are occasions when it's appropriate to get agreement with someone before making a decision. However, much of the time we have the right to decide without getting permission first.

11. An **unhelpful** belief that can straddle both **aggression** and **non-assertion**. This is not to say that manners are not a good thing, but this belief suggests it is the main thing. Politeness when it masks other aspects of behaviour can get in the way, e.g. I may be polite to you as I take advantage of you or manipulate you. Additionally, if you hold this belief, you may find it hard to interrupt someone who is unfairly taking up all the airtime in a meeting.

12. An **unhelpful aggressive** belief. We do live life to some degree on the basis of reciprocity and want to be treated as we would treat others. Holding this belief, however, maintains a cycle of aggression and retribution and usually results in an escalation of emotions and feelings, 'an eye for an eye', etc. There is a number of more 'adult' ways to let people know that they need to deal with you differently.

13. An **unhelpful unassertive** belief. Holding this belief can make you become self-effacing and too accommodating, going along with others' wishes and rarely meeting your own needs and wants. You become unresponsive, walk away from problems and sweep things under the carpet.

14. An **unhelpful aggressive** belief. It is takes courage and strength to admit to being vulnerable. Pretending to be something other than you are, is rarely being true to yourself. You can turn people away and deny yourself your own emotional needs, become proud, egocentric and not see others as equals or treat them with respect.

15. An **unhelpful non-assertive** belief. You have the right to be you. If you live on the eyelids of someone else, they blink and you fall off. This belief leads to frustration as you strive to be somebody you are not. The emotional cost of having multiple 'masks' is debilitating.

16. An **unhelpful** belief that can straddle both **non-assertion** and **aggression**. Holding this belief nurtures stubbornness. You can become powerless to effect any change. You can be resistent to and angry with a world that does not understand or accept you. You can prevent other people from growing by blocking their desire to develop too.

17. An **enabling assertive** belief. People do not have power over you unless you give it to them. You do not lose self-respect and dignity unless you give it away. You are not always responsible for the situations you find yourself in, but you are responsible for how you behave in those situations.

How can you change beliefs?

Identify the one you want to change
The first thing to do, of course, is to identify which belief you want to change. You then have to decide how motivated you are to want to change. Certain beliefs seem harder to change than others because in some you have invested so much of your life.

We once had the privilege to work in a Women's Shelter in Glasgow; the residents were being offered counselling from us and some other colleagues.

These women had often been living in harsh circumstances and most of them had suffered physically. Remarkably many of these battered women shared a similar belief: 'They were not worthy and therefore deserved what they got.'

We soon discovered that unless they changed this belief about themselves they would always be trapped. There was a reluctance to let go of this belief because they felt their personal history was littered with evidence that this was true.

Although their lives were desperate and they weren't being treated with respect, at least they had a partner who, when they weren't being abusive to them, provided them with food and shelter and some form of affection. To escape being a victim would mean changing their beliefs. Until they could believe they were worth so much more, nothing was going to change.

The story had a happy ending for some, who eventually did change their beliefs about themselves and said goodbye to aggression and humiliation.

Challenge with facts

Beliefs are not *true* and are held at an *emotional* level. Central to any belief change is the challenge you make from your 'adult' you, with facts and information that the 'child' you did not have at the time the belief was formed. Questions to ask are:

- How was the belief formed?
- Where does it come from?
- What do you now know to be true?
- What information do you now have which challenges this belief?

For example, you may have formed a belief at school that you were no good at maths or you were 'thick', and you 'asked stupid questions'. At the time, the teacher who said this may have seemed all-powerful and all-knowing, whereas looking back now, you know that was not the case.

You can challenge this belief by gathering other evidence or information that disproves this belief. You may have gone on to do secondary and tertiary education where you will have succeeded in doing the most involved advanced statistics, operational research, etc.

You may now see your inability to be good at maths to be more associated with other factors than with your capability and ignorance.

Act 'as if'

Another way of changing beliefs is by acting '**as if**' you held a different belief and behaving accordingly. You can then experience positive results by adopting it. The effects of this can be to weaken the old unhelpful belief and install or strengthen the enabling belief you 'adopted'. The payoff of success encourages you to now *decide* to hold that belief.

Examples of enabling beliefs

We do not claim these **enabling** beliefs are necessarily true but if you adopt them as if they *are*, the beliefs will assist you in achieving what you want.

Figure 8.1

I am responsible for my actions and you are responsible for yours.

Genuine understanding only comes from experience.

My needs are important and so are others'.

There are no mistakes or failures, only lessons to learn.

You have to have a dream to make a dream come true.

Expect the best, plan for the worst and prepare to be surprised.

Respect comes from within not from without.

I like myself – even though I am not perfect.

The only person you can really change is yourself.

Everyone has something unique to contribute.

Each human being has the potential to change.

Everyone has all the resources they need, even if it takes a little time to find them.

Everyone lives in their own unique version of the world.

I am as important as other people; others are as important as me.

If you always do what you have always done, you will always get what you have always got.

You get more of what you want when you attend to what others want.

I can forgive myself for making mistakes and being human.

It's OK not to know all the answers.

When we stand up for ourselves with integrity, we gain self-respect and respect from others.

I do not need permission from others to act.

Personal relationships develop more depth when we share our honest reactions and encourage others to do the same.
I can learn from other people and experiences; others can learn from me.

When we express ourselves honestly, we show respect for others by letting them know where and what we stand for and giving them a chance to change their behaviour towards us.

I can stand up for myself without attacking other people.

When we sacrifice our rights, we collude with others to take advantage of us.

I can choose how I behave – I do not have to be 'hooked' by others.

It is OK to be me (in ways that do not remove the rights of others).

I can't always choose the situation, but I can always choose my behaviour.

I don't have to lose for other people to win.

Criticism is information, not a personal attack.

Exercise 8.2: CHANGING BELIEFS FROM UNHELPFUL TO ENABLING

Step 1
Identify an **unhelpful** belief that you want to change.

How do you think you learned this **unhelpful** belief in the first place? Perhaps you inherited it from your early childhood, maybe your mum, dad, brother or sister.

How does it effect your decisions and actions?

With the knowledge you now have, challenge the truth of this belief, e.g. are there times when you know that it's not true? Can you find exceptions to the rule? Are there examples of the exact opposite?

What keeps you holding this unhelpful belief?

When you continue to behave in a certain way it's because you get a benefit from it. If you didn't, you wouldn't continue with that behaviour. Sometimes, it is the 'secondary' benefit – the one not immediately apparent, that entices you to hold on to this behaviour.

> For example, challenging a senior manager's view is a limiting career move.

You may not get what you want by holding this belief but at least you don't experience the pressure to come up with ideas, get palpitating heartbeats or that unpleasant feeling in the pit of your stomach. You don't have to take responsibility for making your ideas work or the fear of looking foolish and being wrong.

Step 2
Choose an enabling belief from the list in **Figure 8.1** that you want to hold instead.

Step 3
What rights will you now give yourself permission to hold?

What rights will you now allow others?

Visualise how you'll behave now you're holding this **enabling** belief.

Step 4
What's the greatest benefit you'll get from holding this new belief – how will it change your life?

Will this new belief be appropriate all the time?

Step 5
Carry your new belief with you in your wallet, phone, pocket, bag.

Start by acting 'as if' you held the new belief. You may not feel it, but you can always act it.

Start small, be assertive in relatively simple contexts, such as asking for things in restaurants or shops where it doesn't feel like a 'life or death' situation.

Remember to reflect on your success. Realise how your new belief is making a difference.

CHAPTER 9
WIN:WIN OUTCOMES

The concept of **win:win** is core to assertion; it ensures that your approach is not just selfishly driven and goes beyond just getting more of what you want for yourself. When you use it as a guiding principle it transforms your relationships and becomes a way of life, e.g. balancing _your_ rights and needs with the rights and needs of _others_.

Conrad had been running his own assertiveness programmes for a couple of years when an opportunity arose to go for an interview with Ken and Kate Back who ran a training partnership and were looking for new associates. Ken and Kate had written a seminal book on assertiveness and were inundated with requests to run their programmes throughout the UK and overseas.

The afternoon Conrad met them he was running a training programme in the Midlands, which went on longer than he had expected. Consequently, he was late for the interview and can remember screeching into their shingle driveway, slamming on the brakes, and managing to stop just inches short of a bay window and two very startled faces.

Ken and Kate were very generous with their time, hospitality and good humour and Conrad soon settled down to discuss the possibility of working with them. Towards the end of their discussion they asked the question Conrad had always found difficult to answer: "How much do you want to earn?" Although he'd given this question a lot of thought as he had thundered down the motorway, he now became less certain. A quick calculation – he thought of his present earnings – and doubled them.

Conrad remembers Ken and Kate taking their time, looking quizzically at each other and thought he had over-egged his opening bid. His heart sank and he suspected he was in for some hard bargaining.

Conrad can't fully remember the next few minutes; even today, they are covered in an embarrassed haze, but he roughly recalls Ken and Kate's words: "We were expecting you to ask for more than that. We think you have a lot to offer the partnership and we're wondering why you're selling yourself short. Would you like to take a few moments to reconsider?"

They finally agreed a figure that both of them considered was a fair return for what Conrad would contribute to the business. Conrad now drove very slowly out of their driveway, stunned but inspired by two people who not only spoke about **win:win**, but walked the talk.

You and I are born to negotiate, just as you and I are born to walk and run. You may not even realise that you are negotiating when you talk to your colleagues, business associates, customers, your children, friends, etc. You are negotiating throughout the day and every day of your life.

When your needs and wants are the same as other people's the interaction is very pleasant and rewarding. However, what happens when your needs and other people's needs are different or may seem to be in conflict?

Problems occur when both parties look out solely for their own interests, with little or no consideration for each other or the longer-term impact of their actions. Negotiations may result in one party getting their ideal result, this time, but at the expense of the other.

As time goes on and the relationship continues you may find that a tit-for-tat approach flourishes and you are both trapped in a cycle of lose – win or lose – lose.

There are five potential outcomes from a negotiation; four outcomes within the matrix and the fifth outside the matrix, **No win:no play**.

I win You lose	I win You win
I lose You lose	I lose You win

What is win:win?

Both parties feel sufficiently satisfied about the outcome as the result meets *enough* of both parties' needs.

Win:win negotiation is about alliance, not conflict, and results in long-lasting and strengthened professional relationships. **Win:win** reduces the tension and stress that is associated with posturing and game playing and develops trust.

No win:no play is the authentic position you convey to another party, the default position, that asserts that you are only interested in negotiating provided the other party is also interested in working for a solution that has mutual benefit. If not, you are prepared to walk away from the negotiation rather then pursue game playing, manipulation or threat.

No win:no play is one of the options within your best/worst case scenarios and is the position that represents an unacceptable, significant loss for you. Interestingly, if that is so, how much are you really losing if you take this position?

Three communication skills are very helpful in getting to **win:win**, so let us have a look at them in turn. They are **questioning, testing understanding** and the **verbal handshake**.

Questioning skills

We think you would be surprised to know that, generally, people do not ask many questions. You can easily test this out by sitting and observing people in everyday conversation.

The overwhelming drive we have as human beings is to give more and more information about our circumstances and ideas without asking others the same. Some of this giving of information is important and necessary but the sheer volume of one-way traffic is questionable and exposes our underlying need to be self-interested.

Asking questions would mark you out as a person interested in others' views and ideas, an essential requisite to achieving win:win.

Broadly speaking, there are two types of questions: **closed**, requiring a 'Yes' or 'No' answer, and **open** questions, which ask for further information.

Closed questions seem to come more naturally to most of us, perhaps because they are more 'me' centred. These types of questions spontaneously trip off our tongue because we generally don't need to give them much thought.

Closed questions:
- are helpful in establishing agreement and confirmation
- check that you understand someone else's position or views.

Closed questions start with:
- Do/did?
- Is?
- Have/has?
- Will/would?
- Are?
- If?
- Can/could?
- May?
- Shall/should?

Open questions demand a degree of self-awareness and a conscious decision to involve the 'other' person. Simply put: you need to engage brain before mouth.

Open questions:
- are more useful in establishing real needs
- open up areas for negotiation and further discussion
- engage the problem-solving part of the brain
- encourage involvement
- 'buy' you time to think.

Open questions start with:
- What?
- How?
- Why?
- When?
- Where?
- Who?
- Tell me?

Testing understanding

Testing understanding is also referred to as 'reflecting', 'mirroring', and sometimes 'summarising'. It is a **closed** type of question.

Testing understanding involves checking what you have heard or think you've heard to bring about clarity and reduce confusion and misunderstanding.

If you want to become a better listener then **testing understanding** is one of the ways you could do it. It gives proof that you *have* been listening and builds rapport and trust.

> For example, *"Sally, did you say that travelling for over 50 minutes to work is a problem for you?"*
>
> *"Yes, that's correct but only if I have to travel in the rush hour."*

The verbal handshake

The **verbal handshake** incorporates elements of **testing understanding** and can unblock the log jam within a negotiation. You can't negotiate successfully unless you are both clear and are in agreement what the negotiation is about. It's particularly useful when:

■ the other party seems to ignore or refuses to acknowledge your needs
■ there is a deadlock, the other party refuses to co-operate with you.

For example, *"I appreciate that you believe we shouldn't make any unnecessary changes that might put the deadline at risk.*

Do you appreciate that I wouldn't be suggesting this amendment if I didn't think it was critical to the client?"

For example, *"I can see that you feel very strongly that you're entitled to a further discount on the price.*

Do you appreciate that if I go any further it means I have no margin to cover the cost of servicing?"

Preparing for win:win

Step 1 – Believe it's possible

In order to have more **win:win** experiences we need to *believe* that **win:win** is possible. In the worst case you may have to adopt an **'As if'** belief if you've never experienced many **win:win** outcomes before. Holding this belief enables you to be courageous, considerate and persistent in the search for a mutual resolution.

Specific beliefs in relation to **win:win** are:

■ a person's needs may be different, but they are still valid for that person
■ my needs are important, so are others'

■ I don't have to lose for others to win
■ there is potential for a **win:win**.

Step 2 – Establish your own real needs and wants

Understand your own needs and wants and think of a *range* of possibilities. Develop a *range* that allows you to be firm while being flexible. Your range gives you a number of options within the discussion and also highlights when the deal is **no win:no play**.

The range might cover your degrees of satisfaction:

■ *"What do I ideally want?"*
■ *"What would I be happy with?"'*
■ *"What would I be sufficiently satisfied with?"*
■ *"My needs are not being met. I also need . . ."*
■ *"Definitely not good for me"*
■ *"Better to offer **no win:no play**".*

When stating your real needs make sure you are clear and specific. You may find you express what you *want* as opposed to what you really *need,* e.g.

■ *"I need some help for ten minutes getting started on the presentation, after that I think I can finish it on my own"*
rather than:
■ *"I want some help doing this."*

Step 3 – Establish others' real needs and wants

Not everyone wants to engage in **win:win,** but fortunately behaviour is catching. When you demonstrate that you are only interested in achieving a **win:win,** others are more likely to adopt the same approach.

One way to do this is to start the negotiation on common ground. Establish what you can agree on, what you hold in common, rather than what keeps you apart.

One of the simplest ways to establish common ground is to explicitly agree what you both need, e.g.

■ *"John, you seem to want the reports submitted on time, I do too.*
■ *In order to make that happen I am asking for a day's notice, whenever possible, so that I have the data ready for you.*
■ *Is that a fair summary of what we both want?"*

Obtaining agreement from the other party stimulates a healthy atmosphere in which to continue the discussion, e.g.

■ *"John, is that is a fair summary? Are you happy to go first and tell me what else is important to you?"*

In any negotiation there are times when your ideas and suggestions are resisted. Your normal reaction may be to push harder, repeat the same information, sometimes in a different way or LOUDER. Others will reciprocate – behaviour is catching!

The smarter, more effective option is to ask **open questions**, get past the obstruction, and understand what the other person's real needs are, e.g.

■ *"Brian, when you say it's too costly, what exactly are we talking about?"* or
■ *"Jill, you said it's not up to standard. In what way does it fall short of what you are expecting?"*

Step 4 – Verbal handshake to encourage acceptance of both parties' needs

After establishing the real needs, you may find that there are few differences between you and it's now easier to reach a mutually satisfactory outcome. At other times, it may seem that one set of needs can be met only at the expense of the other. Unless there is a genuine acknowledgement of needs at this stage, it is unlikely that a win:win solution will evolve.

First of all, you need to:
- check you have understood their real needs and show that you accept them.
- get acceptance from the other party to agree and accept your needs by using the **verbal handshake**.

For example, *"Alice, you have said many times that you want to give the best possible service to our customers. I agree with this.*

Can you accept that I need you to release each of your staff to attend the training so that they fully understand how best to do this?"

Step 5 – Creative thinking

What if-type questions encourage the other party to be creative in finding possibilities to apparently insoluble solutions, e.g.

- *"What if we took this approach?"*
- *"There must be a way round this"'*
- *"If there was a way round this, who would we speak to?"*
- *"How about this as an idea?"*
- *"What could be some possible solutions?"*
- *"Could this be a way forward?"*

In this phase, remember to remain open to possibilities yourself and stay focused on the outcome and not the process or the minutiae unless, of course, the 'devil is in the detail'.

Do not assume that you know what the other party wants, keep focused on the other parties' wants and needs, and keep your own range in mind. Summarise at the end what you have both concluded

You will find functioning with a **win:win** approach builds your self-esteem and confidence, even if the result is not always what you had hoped for. You will be confident you stood up for what you wanted in a way that maximised the chances of success – and that's a leg up for most of us!

Contrast the after-effects of acting with a **win:win** mindset compared with a mindset based on win:lose or lose:lose. You may not only fail to get what you want with win:lose or lose:lose, but may also suffer an even greater loss – one of confidence and self-esteem. It's unlikely that you will have the stomach for a similar intervention with the same enthusiasm.

Exercise 9.1: GETTING TO WIN:WIN

Below is a situation where there is a conflict of needs. What three or four questions would you ask to establish your manager's real needs and a possible win:win?

Situation 1

It's the middle of the week when your manager asks you to prepare a report on the future shape of the business in your region over the next five years – "Nothing too elaborate, mind, but full of facts and recommendations, with the draft ready for me first thing Monday."

Compiling this report will help you have an input not only to the future of the company but also to the future security of your own department. Realistically, it will mean three or four days' intense work for you and your team.

Your team are considerably over-stretched and under-resourced. You have planned a Team Away Day this coming Friday and you've also promised your family that whatever happens you are taking them away for the weekend.

You know your manager thinks well of you and turns to you when things are particularly tight and difficult. You would like to help find a solution.

| **Three or four questions you would ask your manager:** |
| 1. |
| 2 |
| 3. |
| 4. |

CHAPTER 10

SAYING "NO"

Wherever you go, in any social or work context, one of the most difficult things to do is to say "No" or to say it assertively. Many a relationship is ruined; many a manager is doomed to irritation, frustration and overwork because of the inability to say "No" assertively. Time management and life/work balance are thrown out of kilter. Eventually, as in relationships, there is breakdown in health.

Do any of the following seem familiar?

You may be able to say "No" only when you are at the end of your tether because you have allowed things to build up. You say "No" aggressively, which invites further aggression and obduracy.

You may have had sleepless nights and anxious days stoking up the courage to come out and say "No", only to feel guilty and bad about yourself when you do. You may have said "No" but will have said it in an apologetic and rambling way, leaving the other person confused and unsure of what you have said. But in the end you still have to do what you didn't want.

You may have thought you said "No" but never uttered the word "No", resulting in agreeing to do something you never wanted to do.

You may have said "Yes" when you really meant to say "No". Confusing for everyone.

You may have failed to say "No" in a negotiation at the point when your needs were not being met.

In a social context, saying "No" may be appropriate without necessarily giving reasons. In an organisational setting, saying "No" and giving valid reasons is important because saying "No" has implications to relationships, to co-operation, to the culture and ways of working.

Benefits to saying "No"

What are the benefits of saying "No" assertively?

- shows commitment and resolution
- earns respect
- displays self-belief
- sets up a balanced negotiation
- allows you to orchestrate win:win negotiations where the other person doesn't acknowledge your needs and wants to steamroller over them
- maintains your psychological and physical health
- creates better time management
- gives you your life back.

The first question to ask yourself when you are considering saying "No" is the question of rights – "Do I believe I have I the right to say 'No' in this situation?"

If the answer is "Yes" and you need to say "No", then the *'No' Sandwich* will give you the structure and guidance to say it in a way that maintains your self-respect and maximises the chance of keeping the relationship with the other person intact.

The 'No' Sandwich

The 'No' Sandwich is rarely used as an 'end stop'. It works well as a staging point, a 'launching pad' to generate win:win possibilities. The 'No' Sandwich works because:

- you are seen to be listening, and to be understanding
- you are seen to be firm yet flexible
- you are clear and leave no room for ambiguity
- you are given respect as a result

■ you place the responsibility for action, etc. where it belongs

■ you are seen to be positive rather than negative

■ you open up the dialogue to a more constructive negotiation.

The 'No' Sandwich steps

Step 1

Acknowledge/empathise with the request by reflecting what you believe you are being asked to agree with or do.

> "Nigel, I can see you're disappointed over the promotion and you think it's unfair that you've been overlooked because I've given the position to John."

Step 2

Say "No" and give the real reason.

(A good way to test whether the reason you are giving is the 'real' one is to ask yourself, "If this were not true would I be prepared to agree?")

You also need to differentiate in your reply, whether you are saying "You can't" (not able) or "You won't" (not willing). The phrase you use will have a very different impact on the other person.

> "No, I won't be recommending you for promotion yet as I think John is more deserving as he has reached Level 3 and has achieved the standard of performance I wanted."

Step 3

Say what you are prepared to do this time/in the future and offer a win:win.

> "Nigel, I value the hard work you do and am more than happy to talk again when you have completed Level 3 to see how we can further your career."

Your "No" may not be welcome news for the other person. After all, they had hoped for a "Yes" or agreement of some kind. They therefore may object with all sorts of comments. The important thing for you to do is reaffirm your original reason and do not be tempted to add another one – this just weakens your stand. You can change how you phrase it but keep the intent the same.

Use the person's name whenever you can to reply.

Ensure that your body language is congruent with the message – pay attention to an 'earthed' position, with firm eye contact and delivered with an even tone, slightly slower than you would normally speak.

The 'No' Sandwich: another example
Acknowledge/empathise
> *"Brenda, I appreciate that you've got several points to contribute and they're often good ideas."*

Say "No" and give the real reason
> *"No, I don't agree that gives you permission to keep interrupting me. I think that shows a lack of respect for me and my views."*

What you are prepared to do – point to the future
> *"In future, let me finish what I have to say and then I'll be happy to listen to you."*

Exercise 10.1: SAYING "NO"
Take a situation that occurred in the past where you had the right to say "No" and didn't.

1. Write down what you would say in each of the steps of the 'No' Sandwich.
2. Ensure that you are giving the real reason, and know how to sustain it.
3. Ensure you have a future orientation to the last step.

Acknowledge/empathise	
Say "No" and give the real reason	
Say what you are prepared to do – point to the future	

Rehearse it with a friend or colleague by telling them briefly about the situation.

4. Invite your friend/colleague to give you practice at saying "No". Ask them to pose the question as if they were the other person and when you respond assertively encourage them to throw objections your way in an attempt to steer you from your "No".
5. Remain firm and fair, true to the real reason and notice how repeating the real reason has the desired effect.
6. Be aware of your non-verbal behaviour, particularly pausing and slowing down.

Exercise 10.2: SAYING "NO" AND GETTING TO WIN:WIN

Take a situation that might occur in the future where you'll need to negotiate with someone and may need to say "No" in order to get to a win:win. The steps below will help you to structure how you prepare for a win:win.

You can then practise it with a friend or colleague by telling them briefly about the situation. You can ask them to act as if they were the 'other person' so you can have actual practice at delivering what you've written and responding to what they say.

1. **State your needs clearly**
   Write down your needs and what you'd be sufficiently happy with.

....

....

....

2. **Encourage others to state their needs. Ask open questions**
   What are the questions you need to ask to clarify their needs?

....

....

....

3. **Get acknowledgement of your needs and acknowledge theirs – the verbal handshake**
   How would you word the verbal handshake?

....

....

....

4. **Create 'what if' options or invite the other party to come up with alternatives – 'creative thinking'**
   What options can you suggest that would lead to a win:win?

5. **If it's appropriate, say "No" in order to establish a position from which to negotiate.**
   How would you word the 'No' Sandwich to show you're looking for a win:win?

....

....

....

6. **Having said "No", go back to Step 4.**

....

....

....

CHAPTER 11
MEETING BEHAVIOURS

You may find you have no difficulties in one-to-one discussions but act differently when placed in a meeting environment. Normally, you have no difficulty speaking up and giving your point of view, but in a meeting are more reticent.

In **Part 2, Chapter 19 'Contributing to Meetings'** we help you to fully prepare yourself for a meeting. Here we introduce you to specific *verbal behaviours* that will help you to contribute effectively.

Verbal behaviours to use

1. **Proposing** – specifies what needs to be *done* clearly and concisely in the form of an *action*-oriented idea. This is made in a form of a *statement*.

   "In my view I think we should talk to . . ."
   "I propose we go to lunch . . ."
   "As I see it, we should make recommendations . . ."

2. **Suggesting** – puts forward ideas and courses of action with a *question*. Although the idea may be the same as **proposing,** by shaping it in the form of a question it makes the idea more appealing and often less likely to be resisted.

   "Should we set new targets?"
   "Could we use more staff?"
   "How about introducing a revised procedure?"

3. **Seeking ideas** – draws people into the meeting and stimulates action-oriented ideas from others.

   "Sarah, how do you think you should go about it?"

"What's going to be the best way to handle them?"
"Anyone got any ideas how we should proceed?"

4. **Supporting** – lets others know what you agree with or support. Supporting creates a creative and win:win atmosphere. Using it also builds alliances and encourages others to support you.

   "I think that's a good idea."
   "I agree with Jon's idea that . . ."
   "That sounds an excellent thing to do."

5. **Building** (on other people's ideas) – developing others' ideas and courses of action, expanding them further and adding to them. Demonstrates you are listening and creates a win:win atmosphere.

   "That's a good idea and then we could go on to re-plan the schedule as well."
   "As you say, we can make a presentation and then let the customer try out the new system."
   "Nice one; and then we could push it out company wide."

6. **Stating differences** – different points of view can lead to a better result. So make them and keep them in proportion. Avoid using the word 'disagree' – it is an emotive 'red rag' of a word. People hear the word 'disagree' and then work out how they are going to disagree with *you* rather than listening to your point of view.

   "I see it differently because . . ."
   "I agree with . . . and have some doubts about . . ."
   "I don't think that is the right course of action."

7. **Seeking information or clarification** – this verbal behaviour is different from *seeking ideas*, which is about *action*; this behaviour is about *information*.

"What is your view on?"
"How does that fit in to what you believe?"
"When you said . . . what were you thinking about?"

8. **Giving information** – giving new or additional information or an explanation. We have to give information to make decisions. Reflect on your own behaviour whether there is a good balance between seeking and giving information. There are no absolutes, but how frequently do you ask questions?

    "They always react the same way."
    "I spoke to them yesterday and they said they love it."
    "Our current overdraft has just leaped to £100k."

9. **Testing understanding** – replaying back another's comment with the aim of ensuring you and they have common understanding.

    "So am I right in thinking that what you want us to do is . . . ?"
    "If I have understood correctly what you are suggesting is we go for broke?"
    "When you said 'x' was important did you mean . . . ?"

10. **Summarising** – frequent summaries allow decisions and action to be understood and lends clarity to what has been said. They can be done in statement or question form.

    "We have discussed the problem with the flues, the cost of repair, who is taking responsibility and when they will be repaired."

    "Can I recap what we have covered? John is going to Blackpool, Sally is returning to Cardiff and we are all meeting up together next Thursday in Edinburgh."

11. **Signalling** – is a technique to make people aware of what you are going to say before you say it. Signalling can be extremely useful if you normally have difficulty breaking into a

discussion or you would like to get people's attention to what you want to say.

"I'd like to ask a question: Tom, what did you . . ."
"Can I clarify what we have agreed: Do we really want . . ."
"I'd like to throw in an idea – before we go any further I'd recommend . . ."

12. **Stating how you feel** – is a technique to explain to others what's happening to you emotionally. The use of this technique can unblock opposition, sponsor honesty and create trust and openness.

"There's a part of me that wants to agree with you, and there is another part that is reluctant to because . . ."

"I feel like I am being manipulated when I thought we had agreed to be open with each other . . ."

Below is an exercise in identifying various kinds of **verbal behaviours**. See if you can recognise them. Once you do, you are in good position to *choose* to use them in meetings and other conversations.

Exercise 11.1: VERBAL BEHAVIOURS

Below is a script of a meeting between three people, Alice, Ben and Charles, who are working on the Cornwall Project. The script is a continuous conversation between the three of them.

The example given is an actual discussion and does not suggest this is the way to conduct a meeting – it is merely illustrative of the verbal behaviours.

Follow their conversation and identify which verbal behaviour you think each of them uses, e.g. whether they are **seeking ideas, giving information**, etc.

We have identified the first 'verbal contribution' from Alice as an example of seeking information.

No.	Person	What they said	Type of verbal behaviour?
1.	Alice	*"What time is it?"*	....
2.	Ben	*"Five o'clock; or it was the last time I looked."*	....
3.	Alice	*"What are we going to do now?"*	....
4.	Ben	*"I think we should just pack up and go home."*	....
5.	Charles	*"That's the best idea I've heard all day."*	....
6.	Alice	*"On the other hand, we could stay and work."*	....
7.	Ben	*"Yes, but they'll turn the power off soon."*	....
8.	Charles	*"And we could stay and sort out the Cornwall account."*	....
9.	Ben	*"No way!"*	....
10.	Charles	*"Why not?"*	....
11.	Ben	*"Because I'm up to here with the Cornwall account."*	....
12.	Alice	*"The Boss always keeps his eye on it."*	....
13.	Charles	*"Their overdraft has gone into overdrive I noticed the other day."*	....

14. Alice   *"Mine's looking pretty sick
at the moment."*   ....

15. Ben   *"Are you saying you've got no money?"*   ....

16. Alice   *"Jennifer bought a secondhand Ferrari
yesterday."*   ....

17. Charles *"This is getting us nowhere. How about
discussing the Cornwall account?"*   ....

18. Alice   *"Fine, then we could go on to discuss
your boss's problems …"*   ....

19. Charles *"But he might hear us."*   ....

20. Alice   *"Well, how do we get round this one?"*   ....

21. Ben   *"Well, here's an idea: we could whisper."*   ....

22. Alice   *"Great, the consensus seems to be that
we all stay here, discussing our bosses,
in the dark, whispering."*   ....

23. Charles *"So what do you think?"*   ....

24. Alice   *"I think it's the daftest idea
since bubble cars."*   ....

25. Charles *"No, it isn't!"*   ....

26. Ben   *"I have a proposal to make that we stop
this conversation and go home."*   ....

27. Alice   *"Absolutely."*   ....

28. Ben   *"Before we do, I must confess to having
a niggling doubt about whether we are all
serious about the project."*   ....

29. Charles *"I am glad you said that, I had that feeling
as well."*   ....

30. Ben   *"If that's so, what shall we do about it?"*   ....

Our answers

1. **Alice**   *"What time is it?"*
'Seeking information' – through a question

2. **Ben**   *"Five o'clock; or it was the last time I looked."*
'Giving information'

3. **Alice**   *"What are we going to do now?"*
'Seeking action ideas'

4. **Ben**   *"I think we should just pack up and go home."*
'Proposing' – an action idea in the form of a statement

5. **Charles** *"That's the best idea I've heard all day."*
'Agreeing' with the proposed course of action

6. **Alice**   *"On the other hand, we could stay and work."*
'Suggesting' another course of action

7. **Ben**   *"Yes, but they'll turn the power off soon."*
'Stating differences' and a problem

8. **Charles** *"And we could stay and sort out the Cornwall account."*
'Building' – taking Alice's idea further (see 6)

9. **Ben**   *"No way!"*
'Stating differences' – a blocking tactic

10. **Charles** *"Why not?"*
    'Seeking information' – asking a question

11. **Ben** *"Because I'm up to here with the Cornwall account."*
    'Giving information' – the start of an information spiral

12. **Alice** *"The Boss always keeps his eye on it."*
    'Giving information' – more information

13. **Charles** *"Their overdraft has gone into overdrive I noticed the other day."*
    'Giving information' – more information

14. **Alice** *"Mine's looking pretty sick at the moment."*
    'Giving information' – more information

15. **Ben** *"Are you saying you've got no money?"*
    'Testing understanding' of what Charles said (see 13)

16. **Alice** *"Jennifer bought a secondhand Ferrari yesterday."*
    'Giving information' although a non-sequitur

17. **Charles** *"This is getting us nowhere. How about discussing the Cornwall account?"*
    'Suggesting' – an action idea in the form of a question

18. **Alice** *"Fine, then we could go on to discuss your boss's problems."*
    'Building' – developing Charles' action ideas further

19. **Charles** *"But he might hear us."*
    'Stating differences'

20. **Alice** *"Well, how do we get round this one?"*
    'Seeking ideas from others'

21. Ben   *"Well, here's an idea, we could whisper."*
            'Signalling + proposing' – an action idea in the form of
            a statement

22. Alice   *"Great, the consensus seems to be that we all stay here,
            discussing our bosses, in the dark, whispering."*
            'Summarising'

23. Charles *"So what do you think?"*
            'Seeking information not ideas'

24. Alice   *"I think it's the daftest idea since bubble cars."*
            'Difficulty stating' – the start of a mini disagreeing spiral

25. Charles *"No, it isn't!"*
            'Difficulty stating'

26. Ben   *"I have a proposal to make that we stop this conversation
            and go home."*
            'Signalling + proposing'

27. Alice   *"Absolutely."*
            'Supporting'

28.   Ben *"Before we do I must confess to having a niggling doubt
            about whether we are all serious about the project."*
            'Stating feelings' + 'Stating differences'

29. Charles *"I am glad you said that, I had that feeling as well."*
            'Supporting'

30. Ben   *"If that's so, what shall we do about it?"*
            'Seeking ideas'

We referred at the beginning of this chapter to what might be your general experience of meetings. If you want to change your behaviour, shorten your meetings and make them more productive, you now have the verbal tools to do that.

Meetings that . . .
go round in circles
take far longer than they should do
have nothing decided at the end
    . . . do so because few people are using any of the verbal behaviours, **Proposing**, **Suggesting** or **Seeking ideas**.

Remember that the intention of assertive behaviour is to bring about **win:win**. Attending a meeting is not an exercise in personal power. *Listen* as well as give, *ask* as well as tell, *support* as well as state problems.

THE TOOLBOX:
A CONCLUSION

We have shared with you the essential tools associated with assertion that we believe make a difference in many of the situations you come across in the workplace. There are no mistakes, only lessons. Growth is a process of trial and error and experimentation. The failed experiments are as much a part of the process as the experiment that ends up working.

You will see in **Part 2** how these tools are used in specific work-related situations.

However, you can use these tools just as effectively in the myriad other social contexts you face. If you use any one of them they will bring about positive change.

As practitioners we always want feedback, what worked and what didn't.

Remember, whatever you do there is **no failure, only feedback.**

PART 2

WORK STATIONS

A step-by-step guide in how to deal with some of the most common situations that you face during your working life

CHAPTER 12

HANDLING AGGRESSION

Introduction

In this chapter we focus on how to be assertive with people whose behaviour you would describe as aggressive.

Throughout this book we have referred to difficult behaviour you come across in many work-related situations, but we still feel it would be useful to devote one entire chapter to this issue because we get asked about it time and time again.

Aggressive behaviour at work is often characterised by blaming others, showing contempt and being hostile, attacking or patronising. It is based on the belief that the aggressor's opinions and needs are more important than anybody else's. Indeed, many times your views or needs are not tolerated or allowed to be heard.

Unlike an assertor, the aggressor stands up for their own rights but they are unconcerned or even dismissive of other people's rights. They will also seek to enhance themselves at the expense of others and often put people down.

No one behaves aggressively all the time, although it may feel like it sometimes! People are more likely to react aggressively when they feel under threat, out of control or want to win at all costs.

Remember, aggressive behaviour towards you can continue only if you allow it. While we're not suggesting you send your temperamental colleague to sit on the 'naughty step', you may want to take a good hard look at what it is that you're doing or not doing that allows them to remain aggressive and off-hand towards you.

There are many ways of handling aggression and this chapter offers you some of the most useful ones.

We'd like you to think about how you currently deal with aggressive behaviour from others – you may have a particular person in mind – and ask if you feel any of these

struck dumb and unable to say anything;

humiliated by the way they talk to you;

angry that you just can't stand up to them;

scared of *any* confrontation;

frightened that others might believe their accusations;

fear that they may get physical and start throwing things;

resentful that they're allowed to get away with it;

anxious that they may make a rash decision without thinking through the consequence;

irritated that they don't seem to understand the damning effect of their behaviour on the rest of the department;

retaliatory;

sanctimonious that ultimately they will lose and *you* will win.

Do you find yourself saying any of the following?

"Help! I don't know what to say."

"Go away, please just go away."

"If they don't change, I'm going to leave."

"I don't deserve this. It's not fair; what will others be thinking of me?"

"Oh no, someone might get hurt and it might be me."

"Why doesn't somebody stop them?"

"If they continue down this path, they're going be sorry."

"Why can't they just leave it? Otherwise we're all headed for disaster."

"Who the hell do they think they are?"

"Just wait, I'll really show 'em up. That's the only way to get through to them."

"They're on a path of self destruction – I can't wait!"

Solution steps – please allow 20 minutes to complete these steps

In order to handle aggression assertively, follow the steps below one by one. You need to allow yourself a quiet solitary 20 minutes to perform these steps today and then a further quiet 20 minutes when you can. Before you start, have a pen and notepad handy.

Step One – Visualising how you want it to be
Imagine in your mind's eye that:
Someone is behaving aggressively towards you and you're handling it well. You're beginning to unlock the possibilities of a future win:win.

......What do you see happening?
......See your posture, facial expression, your gestures.
......Listen to your voice, the tone, particularly the speed and pauses.
......Listen to the tone of the conversation. What is being said?
......See the effect of your assertion gradually defusing the other
　　　person's aggression.
......How does that make you feel?

Step Two – Beliefs
The following beliefs will underpin and support your behaviour in the discussion. Read them through twice.

I'm as important as others and others are as important as me.
When I stand up for myself with integrity I gain self-respect and respect from others.
Confrontation can be healthy and clear the air.
I can choose how I feel and others choose how they feel.
I can choose how I respond, I don't have to be 'hooked' by them.
I can't always choose the situation, but I can always choose my behaviour.
I don't have to lose for others to win.
I can stand up for myself without attacking them.
Other people are capable of changing.
My needs are important, so are theirs.

Then choose the one that you believe will support you most in handling this aggression. Write it down on your notepad.

Step Three – Rights
Yours
The following list of rights will provide you with the confidence you need to behave assertively while handling aggression. Read them through twice.

I have the right to look after myself physically and emotionally.
I have a right to walk away.
I have the right to be the judge of my own worth, my use of my time and my resources.
I have the right to make mistakes, because I'm not perfect.
I have the right to express my feelings, ideas and opinions, which may be different from others.
I have the right to have these listened to and respected, not necessarily agreed with, but accepted as valid for me.
I have the right to deal with others without being dependent on them for approval.
I have the right to say "No" and refuse unreasonable requests.
I have the right to express anger constructively.
I have the right to seek help/support from my boss/HR, etc.

Then choose the one *right* that you want to give yourself most – because if you do, it will entitle you to the respect you deserve. Write it down on your notepad.

Others'
The following list of other people's rights will ensure you behave assertively in response to their aggression.
Read them through twice.

They have the right to be treated with respect.
They have the right to express their feelings, which may be different from mine.
They have the right to have needs that may be different from mine.
They have a right to have these taken seriously and be accepted as valid for them.
They have a right to be consulted about decisions that affect them.

They have the right to refuse unreasonable requests.
They have the right to ask for what they want.
They have the right to give constructive criticism.
They have the right to make mistakes every now and again.
They have the right to express anger constructively.

Then choose the one *right* that you need to give others most – because if you do, it will entitle others to the respect they deserve from you. Write it down on your notepad.

Step Four – Self-talk
Below are some of the things that you need to say to yourself in order to programme yourself for an effective discussion.

- ■ *"When I handle their aggression well it can lead to a strengthening of our relationship."*
- ■ *"Today's aggression may have been triggered by something totally unrelated to our work."*
- ■ *"I can show that I'm prepared to listen."*
- ■ *"Some of what they say may be valid. I can acknowledge that."*
- ■ *"I can stay calm and state my position."*
- ■ *"I can handle it and show that I want to find a win:win."*
- ■ *"I can say 'No' and give my reasons why."*
- ■ *"I can ask questions to understand the real issue."*
- ■ *"If their abusive behaviour continues, I can walk away from it."*
- ■ *"I can seek help from HR, my boss."*
- ■ *"If they don't like me, it's OK."*

Write down below any more self-talk that you believe will help you get the result you want in handling this aggression.

....
....
....

Finally, choose one piece of self-talk that will be your *mantra* – something you can repeat again and again to yourself as a way of reinforcing your assertive behaviour. Write it down on your notepad.

Step Five - Behavioural tips to apply when handling aggression

Below is a list of non-verbal and verbal tips to get the result you want in this discussion.

(The aim of these behavioural tips is to first handle the aggression and then attend to the problem.)

Non-verbal tips

Pause to consider what's being said by the aggressor.
Take a deep breath.
Stretch the palms of your hands and your finger tips to relax yourself.
Take another deep breath.
Stand or sit upright with both feet on the ground in the 'earthed' position (legs uncrossed).
Slow down the pace by talking slowly and firmly.
Open posture and open gestures.
Make eye contact with them.
Use person's name.
End your sentences and questions in a lower tone of voice.

Verbal tips

If the aggression comes across to you as a short, sharp 'put down', return the 'put down' with a question to stop them in their tracks, e.g. *"What makes you say that?"* or *"What evidence do you have to support that?"* or *"What makes you so sure you're right?"* or *"What makes you so sure I am wrong?"* or *"What makes you think I'm lying?"* or *"What makes you believe I should have done?"* or *"What makes you think we can't?"*

If the aggression is more sustained, show empathy towards the feelings they're expressing, e.g. *"I can appreciate from your tone that you feel very angry about what's happened."*

Acknowledge any valid points they are making, e.g. *"I accept that she wasn't at all happy about the way things were left."*

Listen and show that you're prepared to listen, e.g. *"Mmmm, I see."*

When you're unsure about what's being said or you want to slow the conversation down, use *Testing understanding*, e.g. *"Are you saying that . . . ?"* or *"Is this what you see as being most important . . . ?"*

Ask *open questions* to engage their thinking so that you can encourage them to be assertive, e.g. *"What can we do about this?"*, *"What other options are there?"*, *"What prevents us from taking further action?"*

Ask about how things can be different in the future, e.g. *"What can we do to stop this happening again?"*, *"So how will you organise yourself differently in the future?"*, *"What result do we want from now on?"*

If they ignore your questions, state what you want to happen next, e.g. *"I want to stop talking about this now and discuss it with you this afternoon when the deadline isn't hanging over us."*

Then *signal* that you're looking for a *win:win*, e.g. *"I'm looking for a solution that we both feel comfortable with."*

If the aggression continues unabated refer to the discrepancy in their behaviour, e.g. *"Mike, you said you were fed up with the way things were going and that you wanted changes. Now you're telling me you're not prepared to sit down and find a solution. Let's put some time aside later today to sort this properly."* If they dismiss what you say and their aggression continues, tell them how you feel and the effects of their behaviour on the business, e.g. *"Mike, when you continue to interrupt me like this I feel very angry. The effects of your behaviour on the rest of the team are seriously going to put in jeopardy the deadline. I'd like you to meet with me later day to sort this out properly."*

If they still refuse to calm down, step up your assertion and tell them what you will do if they don't change their behaviour, e.g. *"Mike, if you continue with this behaviour I shall have to call personnel/your boss/put the phone down/call security. Now I don't want to do that so please let's agree to sort this out this afternoon."*

You can call a halt to the proceedings, e.g. *"Mike, we're not going to sort this out in this way. I suggest you call me when we've both had a chance to think about it further."*

Finally, you may choose at any time during the proceedings to refer to the 'relationship' between you and them and remove the work context, e.g. *"Mike, I suspect that your anger with me today has not got anything to do with missing the deadline, but more to do with something going wrong in the relationship between us. I believe it would be very useful if we could discuss why you and I are arguing so much."*

Choose two or three behavioural tips from this list that you believe will work for you. Write them down on your notepad and place this where it will be a continual reminder for you.

CHAPTER 13

PRODUCTIVE APPRAISALS

Introduction

In this chapter we identify how to assertively conduct an appraisal and how to be confident when you're the one being appraised.

Whatever you think about the relevance of an appraisal system, most companies operate them to some degree. Some managers and some organisations view these as a genuine opportunity to develop the potential in their people. Some view it as a necessary evil and resent having to give up valuable time just to please the HR department, or go through the motions because it's 'company policy'.

Whatever your own personal view of appraisals there are some tools and techniques to use to ensure that you get the most from the opportunity.

Appraisals or Performance Development Reviews are generally held bi-annually or annually. You may find that there is an expectation that a certain amount of paperwork is completed prior to and during the appraisal interview. We recommend that you prepare well – 'preparation is everything'.

We'd like you to think about an appraisal interview that may be coming up and ask if you feel any of these.

Fear that there will be conflict of some kind.

Frustrated because you think the whole appraisal process is a tick-in-the-box for HR and a complete waste of time.

Afraid that they'll think you're just biased.

Anxious that it will mean confronting performance issues.

Resigned to the fact that you will not have an opportunity to state your case.

Annoyed because you think you might receive unfair criticism.

Frightened that you might get some bad news about changes within the department that might adversely affect you.
Resentful because you believe whatever promises are made by your manager, nothing will actually happen.
Disenchanted with the whole process.

Do you find yourself saying any of the following?

"Oh no, I remember the last time I conducted an appraisal with them, this one's bound to be worse."

"I know what will happen, they'll accuse me of favouritism. What am I going to say?"

"If I had my way I'd just shelve the whole appraisal process and spend more time on team-building events."

"If they start comparing me with 'so and so' I'll just tell them what 'so and so' really gets up to behind their back."

"I'm the only one who prepares properly – my manager/my member of staff doesn't take this seriously."

"What if I'm told that the department's going to make cut backs next year? I might be out of a job!"

"I can see it now: they'll describe all the wonderful training that I'm entitled to, but they've no intention of making it a reality."

"I've better things to do with my time than going through this ritual."

Solution steps – please allow 20 minutes to complete these steps

In order to conduct an appraisal assertively and be confident when you're the one being appraised, follow the steps below one by one. You need to allow yourself a quiet solitary 20 minutes to perform these steps today and then a further quiet 20 minutes just prior to the actual appraisal event. Before you start, have a pen and notepad handy.

Step One - Visualising how you want it to be

Imagine in your mind's eye that either:
you're conducting an appraisal and it's going well
or
you are sitting in your own appraisal and it's going well.

......What do you see happening?
......See your posture, facial expression, your gestures.
......Listen to your voice, the tone, particularly the speed and pauses.
......Listen to the tone of the conversation - what is being said?
......See the effect of your assertion on the other person.
......How does that make you feel?

Step Two - Beliefs

The following beliefs will underpin and support your behaviour in the appraisal. Read them through twice.

Organisations can provide the means for growth and achievement.
Others pay attention to what you pay attention to.
I can give praise without causing embarrassment.
My future is my responsibility.
I can forgive myself for making mistakes and being human as long as I show a willingness to learn.
There are no mistakes or failures, only lessons to learn.
Confront people's behaviour not them.
People are capable of change.
People are full of potential.
I can be honest with myself, and I can be honest with others too.
My needs are important and so are other people's.

Then choose the one that you believe will support you most in the appraisal. Write it down your notepad.

Step Three - Rights
Yours
The following list of rights will provide you with the confidence you need to behave assertively in the appraisal. Read them through twice.

I have the right for the job to be done to an agreed standard.
I have the right to know what the agreed standard is (before my appraisal).
I have the right to deal with others without being dependent on them for approval.
I have the right that my behaviour/performance is challenged and not my personality.
I have the right to express my views, which may be different from others'.
I have the right to have my opinions listened to.
I have the right to disagree on something.
I have the right to be supported by my boss.
I have the right to have the correct tools to do my job effectively.
I have the right to ask questions and know the reasons why.

Then choose the one *right* that you want to give yourself most – because if you do, it will entitle you to the respect you deserve. Write it down on your notepad.

Others'
The following list of other people's rights will ensure you behave assertively towards them in the appraisal. Read them through twice.

They have the right to know what's expected of them.
They have the right to express their views, which may be different from mine.
They have the right to be listened to.
They have the right to be kept informed about future changes that may affect them.
They have the right to be provided with adequate training in order to perform their job sufficiently well.
They have the right to my support and guidance.
They have the right to know what they do well.
They have the right to know what they need to improve.

They have the right to know of any future changes that may affect my performance.
They have the right to be respected.

Then choose the one *right* that you need to give others most – because if you do, it will entitle others to the respect they deserve from you. Write it down on your notepad.

Step Four – Self-talk
Below are some of the things that you need to say to yourself in order to programme yourself for a successful appraisal.

- *"This is an opportunity – so take it in both hands."*
- *"This a valuable use of my time."*
- *"There'll probably be some differences of opinion. I can stay calm and acknowledge that we both see things differently."*
- *"I can tell them what I thought they did well and the reasons why."*
- *"I can explain the areas they need to improve in and ask them what they need from me in order to meet these standards."*
- *"If they start making excuses, I can be firm and question what they say."*
- *"I can ask about the future of the department. They may not be able to tell me everything there is to know, but they have a responsibility to keep their staff sufficiently informed."*
- *"I can tell them what resources and training I need to do my job well. They have a right to listen and agree or disagree and a responsibility to provide me with adequate help/training."*
- *"I want to know what I've done well, what I need to develop and how my boss sees my future."*
- *"Anything extra I'm asking for will benefit me and the company."*

Write down below any more self-talk that you believe will help you get the result you want at this appraisal.

....

....

....

Finally, choose one piece of self-talk that will be your *mantra* – something you can repeat again and again to yourself as a way of reinforcing your commitment before the appraisal. Write it down on your notepad.

Step Five – Behavioural tips to apply at the appraisal
Below is a list of non-verbal and verbal tips to get the result you want at this appraisal.

Non-verbal tips
Smile when greeting the other person.
Make eye contact with them.
Use the person's name.
Sit in an 'earthed' position, e.g. both feet firmly on the ground.
Keep your gestures open and at waist height.
When asking a question maintain an upright sitting position.
When answering a question take your time, nod thoughtfully before you respond.
Keep a relaxed facial expression.
End your sentences in a lower tone of voice.

Verbal tips
Use the first couple of minutes to build rapport by discussing something of mutual interest, e.g. the status of a particular project or a customer who is of interest to both of you.
Explain that this is an important time together and that you've prepared for it. Show that you've made notes.
Use *open questions* to explore areas of interest, or concern, or to find out the motives behind actions, e.g. *"When you did that what was your thinking?* or *"What had you intended by doing x?"*
Test understanding frequently, e.g. *"So you really enjoyed the challenge and learnt a lot from working with . . . ?"* or *"Are you saying you want me to take on further responsibility?"*
Summarise before you move onto another topic, e.g. *"We've agreed that you'll learn more about the job by shadowing Tom. That'll start this Monday. We'll get together at the end of each week to review how successful you've been."*
If you receive resistance to your opinions, use the *verbal handshake*

to gain acknowledgement to your views, e.g. *"I understand that you think this is unnecessary and taking up too much time. Do you appreciate that this is the standard we've agreed to work to within the team?"*

Be specific with your praise, e.g. *"I noticed when you speak with our clients you always leave them reassured."*

Be specific with your criticism, e.g. *"When you leave out the customer account details, it takes the warehouse twice as long to process the order and this is losing us customers."*

Ask how they see it: *"What's your view on this?"*

If they try to steer you away from your point of view use the 'No' Sandwich, e.g.

"I can see you don't agree with me because it hasn't worked for you in the past.

No, I'm keen to give it a trial run because circumstances have changed and we now have a great opportunity.

Next time I propose we make a change that you disagree with, talk to me about it and if I can agree with you I will."

or

"I appreciate that you think I didn't contribute enough.

No, I feel differently in that I was the one who instigated the review and initiated many of the actions that were successful.

It's clear to me next time I need to document my actions so you can see what I've done."

Place emphasis on what you're going to do or you've agreed between you, e.g. *"I'll email you this before close of business today,"* or *"I'll apply for this tomorrow."*

Keep **win:win** in mind throughout the appraisal, e.g. *"I'd like to take on more responsibility and feel in order to do so I need to attend the training that's available"* or *"Before I can give you a grade increase I need to see you achieving the standards we've agreed for that grade."*

Choose two or three behavioural tips from this list that you believe will work for you. Write them down on your notepad and place this where it will be a continual reminder for you.

CHAPTER 14

MANAGING YOUR BOSS

Introduction

In this chapter we provide you with advice on how to gain respect from your boss, particularly how to gain their acknowledgement of your efforts.

Unless we work for ourselves we all report to someone else. This person may be easily accessible but not very communicative or they may be located a million miles away but very approachable.

Just because someone has been appointed as a manager it doesn't necessarily mean that they are well suited to the role. Some managers find it difficult to make decisions and take risks, while others are natural-born leaders.

Whatever type of boss you have, there are some tools and techniques to use to ensure that you get the most from the working relationship with your boss.

However, no amount of technique will bolster a flagging relationship; you need to build goodwill between the two of you over weeks and months. One way you could think about this is to imagine you were the boss; this will give you some clues about how you build the relationship on a more permanent basis. What would you want from someone like yourself, e.g. most bosses don't like unpleasant surprises; they like to be kept informed. Do you keep them informed?

We'd like you to think about a one:one meeting or conference call you may be planning to have with your boss to review your work and ask if you feel any of these

A sense of dread that you're in for some bad news.
Concerned that they don't think you're pulling your weight.

Worried that they might just think you're not 'up to it'.
Frustrated because they never give you any feedback.
Helpless because they just don't seem to care.
Afraid they're going to give you more work.
Anxious that they think you're just a trouble maker.
Angry because they can't make a decision!
Frustrated the conversation will be a waste of time.

Do you find yourself saying any of the following?

"What have I done wrong now?"
"It's not fair. They never show any sign of interest so I don't know if they're happy or not."
"The problem with them is they're just never around to know what's going on."
"It's always the same: they agree to what I ask for, but they've no intention of doing anything about it."
"Why can't she see the situation from my point of view?"
"They think I'm difficult to manage; that's why they're always trying to avoid me."
"They'll never agree to it, so what's the use?"
"They're just too scared to rock the boat."
"I will be given little opportunity to say what I think."

Solution steps – please allow 20 minutes to complete these steps

In order to be confident and assertive when you're meeting with your boss, follow the steps below one by one. You need to allow yourself a quiet solitary 20 minutes to perform these steps today. Before you start, have a pen and notepad handy.

Step One – Visualising how you want it to be

Imagine in your mind's eye that your in a one:one meeting with your boss and it's going well.

......What do you see happening?
.......See your posture, facial expression, your gestures.
.......Listen to your voice, the tone, particularly the speed and pauses.
.......Listen to the tone of the conversation – what is being said?
.......See the effect of your assertion on the other person.
.......How does that make you feel?

Step Two – Beliefs
The following beliefs will underpin and support your behaviour in the meeting. Read them through twice.

I can make things happen rather than wait for them to happen.
There are no mistakes or failures, only lessons to learn.
You get more of what you want when you attend to what others want.
It's OK not to know all the answers.
Personal relationships develop more depth when we share our honest reactions and encourage others to do the same.
I don't have to lose for others to win.
My self-respect comes from me, not from others.
My needs are important, so are theirs.
I can stand up for what I believe in without attacking others
I can be honest with myself and I can be honest with others.

Then choose the one that you believe will support you most in your meeting.
Write it down on your notepad.

Step Three – Rights
Yours
The following list of rights will provide you with the confidence you need to gain your boss's respect. Read them through twice.

I have the right to ask for feedback on my performance.
I have the right to know what are the standards of performance.
I have the right to have my opinions listened to.
I have the right to express my views, which may be different from others'.

I have the right to be human and make mistakes and learn from them.

I have the right to say I don't understand and seek clarification.

I have the right to refuse unreasonable requests.

I have the right to think before I answer.

I have the right to support from others in order to perform my job/role well.

I have the right to know about a decision on something that affects me.

Then choose the one *right* that you want to give yourself most – because if you do, it will entitle you to the respect you deserve. Write it down on your notepad.

Others'

The following list of your boss's rights will ensure you behave assertively towards them in the meeting. Read them through twice.

They have the right for work to be done to an agreed standard.

They have the right to give me feedback on my performance.

They have the right to take a reasonable amount of time in coming to a decision.

They have the right to be in full possession of the facts.

They have the right to express their views, which may be different from mine.

They have the right to be listened to.

They have the right to feedback from me.

They have the right to be human and to make mistakes.

They have the right to honesty from me.

They have the right to be supported by their staff.

Then choose the one *right* that you need to give others most – because if you do, it will entitle others to the respect they deserve from you. Write it down on your notepad.

Step Four – Self-talk

Below are some of the things that you need to say to yourself in order to programme yourself for a successful meeting with your boss.

- *"I can show them I care about the business and explain that I want to get things right."*
- *"I can ask them what they think I'm doing well and what I need to improve on."*
- *"I can ask them to be specific rather than accept general comments."*
- *"I can express my view calmly and clearly."*
- *"I can ask them for regular one:one review meetings."*
- *"I can ask them for the support I need and give them as much notice as possible."*
- *"I can acknowledge that they need to weigh up all the pros and cons before they make a decision."*
- *"I can ask them what else they need from me in order to come to a decision."*
- *"I can accept that they have many different pressures on their time."*
- *" I can keep 'win:win' in my head at all times."*

Write down below any more self-talk that you believe will help you get the result you want at this meeting.

....

....

....

Finally, choose one piece of self-talk that will be your *mantra* – something you can repeat again and again to yourself as a way of reinforcing your commitment before the meeting. Write it down on your notepad.

Step Five – Behavioural tips to apply at the discussion
Below is a list of non-verbal and verbal tips to get the result you want.

Non-verbal tips
Smile when greeting your boss.

Make eye contact with them.

Use their name.

Find a comfortable seating position in a chair that gives your back support so you can sit upright and be 'earthed'.

Keep your gestures open and at waist height.

Keep a relaxed, open facial expression.

When asking a question maintain an upright position.

When answering a question take your time, nod thoughtfully before you respond.

End your sentences in a lower tone of voice.

Verbal tips

Prepare *open questions* on issues you think will be discussed, e.g. *"How do you think I can do this differently?"* or *"What leads you to believe that would work better?"*

Look for opportunities to *test* your *understanding*, e.g. *"Are you saying that . . . ?"* or *"Is this how you see it . . . ?"*

If you feel you're not getting the opportunity to make your point of view, *signal* your intention, e.g. *"Would you like to hear my view on that?"* or *"I'd like to make a comment about that."*

Use a *verbal handshake* when appropriate, e.g. *"Mike, I appreciate that you've been doing lots of travelling during these last few weeks and that you haven't had a moment to yourself. Can you see that I've been coping on my own without any clear direction and that what I need most is to schedule some regular one:one time with you?"*

Use language that shows you're looking for a *win:win*, e.g. *"Once I have been shown how I configure the start, I am sure I will be competent at doing the work and produce a good result."*

When you think you need to stand your ground, use the *'No' Sandwich*, e.g. *"I can understand you want me to take on this extra responsibility. I am pleased to know you think so highly of me. No, I believe if I take this work both jobs will suffer as I do not have extra time available. How about we look at some alternatives?"*

Place *emphasis* on what you're going to *do*, e.g.
"I'll provide you with the all the evidence you need" or *"I'll deliver the presentation in a way that captures their imagination."*

Choose two or three behavioural tips from this list that you believe will work for you. Write them down on your notepad and place this where it will be a continual reminder for you.

CHAPTER 15

CO-OPERATIVE COLLEAGUES

Introduction

In this chapter we provide help with regard to being assertive with your colleagues at work.

For instance, there will be people with whom you see eye-to-eye and there will be those you don't. You may feel supported by some and not by others. There will be someone who irritates the hell out of you and another will be your best friend. You may see some as your allies and others as your enemies.

Working relationships are among the most difficult ones to manage: we don't necessarily have the luxury of choosing people we have to work with.

You may want to please in order to appease. When you walk away from facing up to conflict, you sometimes feel resentful that you seem to be carrying the heaviest load and that others are getting away with it. You can feel that your efforts are taken for granted and not reciprocated.

You may look towards your boss as the referee and fixer. In some cases this may have to happen. However, there is much that you can do to create the kind of working environment you want.

Let's remember you are working for the same company and you need to manage these relationships with your colleagues sufficiently well to achieve a happy and healthy working environment. After all, you spend half your waking life at work. If during this time you find yourself irritated, frustrated and not respected, how can you enjoy this time?

We'd like you to think about a difficult relationship you have with a colleague and ask if you feel any of these.

Concerned that they may not like you.

Afraid if you complain they'll see you as a trouble maker.

Nervous that there may be confrontation.

Hopeful someone else will sort out the 'issues'.

Isolated and not part of the team.

Despairing because you're the butt of their jokes.

Cross that they see you as a pushover.

Resentful that they don't pull their weight.

Frustrated that they don't tell you what their real issues are.

Irritated that you're the one who always has to pick up the pieces.

Resigned to leaving if things don't get any better.

Do you find yourself saying any of the following?

"If I say what I really feel, they may not like me and that would be awful."

"I'll just keep to myself in future."

"I know what will happen: they'll get really upset and that'll spoil our relationship."

"If I put my ideas forward, they'll think I'm pushy, trying to undermine them in front of others."

"Oh no, they're just waiting for me to make a mistake."

"They've got it in for me."

"What have I done to deserve this?"

"Why can't everybody else work as hard as me?"

"What's the matter with them? Why can't they say what's on their mind?"

"It's not fair. Why am I always the one who has to sort out the mess?"

"I can't wait to get out of here."

Solution steps – please allow 20 minutes to complete these steps

In order to behave assertively with your colleagues, follow the steps below one by one. You need to allow yourself a quiet solitary 20 minutes to perform these steps today and then a further quiet

20 minutes when you can. Before you start, have a pen and notepad handy.

Step One – Visualising how you want it to be

Imagine in your mind's eye that you're talking face to face with a colleague about a difficult issue. The conversation is going well.

......What do you see happening?
......See your posture, facial expression, your gestures.
......Listen to your voice, the tone, particularly the speed and pauses.
.......Listen to the tone of the conversation – what is being said?
......See the effect of your assertion on the other person.
......How does that make you feel?

Step Two – Beliefs

The following beliefs will underpin and support your behaviour in the discussion. Read them through twice.

Essentially we are all here to do a good job.
It's possible for me to create a good working relationship.
I can be honest *and* respectful in my dealings with others.
Assertion is not about being liked, it's about being respected.
My time is important and so is other people's.
I can stand up for myself without attacking people.
I can make things happen rather than wait for them to happen.
The only person I can really change is myself.
Personal relationships develop more depth when I share my honest reactions and encourage others to do the same.
I choose how I feel – I don't have to be manipulated by others.
I'm responsible for my behaviour, others are responsible for theirs.
I don't have to lose for other people to win.

Then choose the one that you believe will support you most in the discussion. Write it down on your notepad.

Step Three - Rights
Yours
The following list of rights will provide you with the confidence you need to behave assertively during the discussion. Read them through twice.

I have the right to support from my work colleagues.
I have the right to express my views, which may be different from theirs.
I have the right to say "No" without feeling guilty.
I have the right to be listened to.
I have the right to suggest changes.
I have the right to deal with others without being dependent on them for approval.
I have the right to be treated with respect.
I have the right to use my time effectively.
I have the right to make requests of others.
I have the right to decline responsibility for other people's problems.

Then choose the one *right* that you want to give yourself most – because if you do, it will entitle you to the respect you deserve. Write it down on your notepad.

Others'
The following list of other people's rights will ensure you behave assertively and not submissively or aggressively towards them in the discussion. Read them through twice.

They have the right to support from me.
They have the right to express their opinions and views, which may be different from mine.
They have the right to be listened to and taken seriously.
They have the right to decline responsibility for my problems.
They have the right to an explanation.
They have the right to ask for what they want.
They have the right to be their own self – this may be different from how I'd like them to be.
They have the right to make mistakes and be responsible for them.

They have the right to refuse unreasonable requests.
They have the right to decide not to assert themselves.

Then choose the one *right* that you need to give others most –
because if you do, it will entitle others to the respect they deserve
from you. Write it down on your notepad.

Step Four – Self-talk
Below are some of the things that you need to say to yourself in order
to programme yourself for an effective discussion.

- ■ *"I don't have to go along with them. I can explain what concerns me."*
- ■ *"What could be some win:wins for us here?"*
- ■ *"If they don't seem to care, I can speak to them and explain why
  they need to accept their responsibility."*
- ■ *"I can praise their behaviours that really help me."*
- ■ *"I can put my points across and ask what people think."*
- ■ *"I can invite others to contribute if they don't speak up."*
- ■ *"If there is a difficult exchange, I can keep calm."*
- ■ *"If they get upset, it doesn't have to spoil our relationship."*
- ■ *"If they ridicule my efforts, it may not be easy but I can be firm
  and deal constructively with any criticism."*
- ■ *"I can say 'No' and give my reasons why."*
- ■ *"I can ask what else they need from me."*
- ■ *"They have the right to make mistakes, but not to keep making
  them."*

Write down below any more self-talk that you believe will help you
get the result you want.

....
....
....

Finally, choose one piece of self-talk that will be your *mantra* –
something you can repeat again and again to yourself as a way of
reinforcing your assertion. Write it down on your notepad.

Step Five – Behavioural tips to apply during the discussion

Below is a list of non-verbal and verbal tips to get the result you want in this discussion.

Non-verbal tips
Smile when greeting the other person.
Make eye contact with them.
Use the person's name.
Sit in an 'earthed' position, e.g. both feet firmly on the ground.
Keep your gestures open and at waist height.
When asking a question maintain an upright sitting position.
When answering a question take your time, nod thoughtfully before you respond.
Keep a relaxed facial expression.
End your sentences in a lower tone of voice.

Verbal tips
Before commencing the discussion show respect for their time by *signalling*, e.g. *"Ben, do you have a few moments? I just need your thoughts on something."*
Signal what you're going to do before you do it, e.g. *"I have a question I'd like to ask,"* or *"I'm unsure about something and thought you might be able to help."*
Ask *open questions* to understand their views, e.g. *"Sarah, what makes you say that?"*
When appropriate use a *verbal handshake*, e.g. *"I understand you believe so and so is correct. Do you acknowledge that I see it in a different way?"*

Stop interruptions by saying their name first and *signalling* your intention, e.g. *"Sarah, I'd like to finish what I'm saying."*
Signal that you're looking for a *win:win* rather than sticking rigidly to your view, e.g. *"I'm looking for a solution that we're both happy with"* or *"I want to achieve something that you're happy with too."*
If the other person tries to steer you away from a *win:win*, use a 'No' *Sandwich*, e.g. *"Paul, I appreciate you think that I'm making much too*

much of a fuss over this. No, I feel differently in that I believe if we don't pay it sufficient attention, it will effect all of us. Next time if you think I'm wrong let's talk about it."

Invite others to speak by saying, *"I'm interested to find out what you feel about . . ."* or *"I'm curious to know more about your thoughts on . . ."*

If you agree with something that's being said, then say so, e.g. *"Yes I agree, that's how I feel too."*

When disagreeing with someone say, *"I see it differently in that I believe . . ."*

When you don't understand something, *test understanding*, e.g. *"When you mentioned xyz what specifically did you mean?"* or *"I'd like to understand better what you meant when you referred to . . ."*

If they're dismissive of what you say, tell them how you feel and the effects of their behaviour, e.g. *"Paul, when you dismiss my attempts to work together, I feel disappointed because I think we could do so much better. I'd like you to reconsider."*

Choose two or three behavioural tips from this list that you believe will work for you. Write them down on your notepad and place this where it will be a continual reminder for you.

CHAPTER 16

HEALTHY CUSTOMER RELATIONSHIPS

Introduction

In this chapter we focus on how you can achieve a healthy and profitable relationship with your customers – one that is based on the assertive principals of win:win.

You may be in credit control, or in customer services. You may be an engineer or technician, or you may be involved in dispatch and delivery, sales ordering or work on a help desk. You may be the sales director of a large corporation or the managing director of your own company.

Many customers are a pleasure to do business with and can even become close friends. Others you may feel were born on an entirely different planet from you and their expectations may be unrealistic. They can be disrespectful, selfish and unwilling to compromise!

Whatever your experience of customers, there's no getting away from the fact that we all need customers to survive.

> *"A customer is the most important visitor on our premises. He is not dependent on us. We are dependent on him. He is not an interruption in our work – he is the purpose of it. We are not doing him a favour by serving him. He is doing us a favour by giving us the opportunity to serve him."* Mahatma Gandhi

This chapter concentrates on the external customer. We acknowledge that customers can also be 'internal' and are due the same respect and attention you would give the external customer.

We'd like you to think about the difficult conversations you have with some of your customers and ask if you feel any of these

Afraid that if you say "No" to their demands, they might go elsewhere.

Fear that if you stand firm and maintain your position, you may later be undermined by your boss.

Worried that the customer might even go and complain about you to your MD and/or the press.

Frightened that they might speak to your other clients.

Resentful that your extra efforts are not being appreciated.

Angry that the relationship feels so one-sided.

Cross that they take up so much of your time.

Blame the sales department for promising too much.

Do you find yourself saying any of the following?

"If I refuse what they're asking, they may not order from us again."

"Whatever I say, they'll demand to speak to 'the manager' and I know my boss will cave in and give them what they want."

"Oh no, they just like complaining! It'll be all over the papers and I could lose my job!"

"I bet they contact our other retailers and then there'll be trouble."

"Don't they realise how much we do for them?"

"I know there'll be nothing wrong; they're nothing but a nuisance."

"They have no right to waste my time like this."

"Who sold them this then? Typical Sales!"

"I'll have to be economical with the truth because I can't give them the real picture."

Solution steps – please allow 20 minutes to complete these steps

In order to behave confidently with your customers, follow the steps below one by one. You need to allow yourself a quiet solitary 20 minutes to perform these steps today and then a further quiet 20 minutes when you can. Before you start, have a pen and notepad handy.

Step One – Visualising how you want it to be

Imagine in your mind's eye that either:

You're sitting in a face-to-face meeting with your customer

or

You're having a phone conversation with them and it's going well.

......What do you see happening?

......See your posture, facial expression, your gestures.

......Listen to your voice, the tone, particularly the speed and pauses.

.......Listen to the tone of the conversation – what is being said?

......See the effect of your assertion on the other person.

......How does that make you feel?

Step Two – Beliefs

The following beliefs will underpin and support your behaviour in the discussion. Read them through twice.

There are no difficult customers, only difficult situations.

I can be honest and respectful in my dealings with others.

I don't have to lose for other people to win.

My time is important and so is other people's.

I can stand up for myself without attacking people.

I choose how I feel – I don't have to be manipulated by others.

I'm responsible for my behaviour; others are responsible for theirs.

Criticism is information, not a personal attack on me.

You get more of what you want when you attend to what others want.

Problems are an opportunity for us to demonstrate outstanding customer service.

It's assertive to say "I'm sorry" if I'm at fault.

Then choose the one that you believe will support you most in the discussion. Write it down on your notepad.

Step Three - Rights
Yours
The following list of rights will provide you with the confidence you need to behave assertively during the discussion. Read them through twice.

I have the right to be treated with respect.
I have the right to refuse unreasonable demands.
I have the right to walk away/put the phone down if the customer is abusive.
I have the right to seek a win:win.
I have the right to say "No" in order to get to a win:win.
I have the right to ask the customer to take responsibility for what they can do to resolve the issue.
I have the right to be supported by management.
I have the right to question or challenge.
I have the right to use my time effectively.
I have the right to give constructive feedback to the sales department about the effect of their sales tactics.

Then choose the one *right* that you want to give yourself most – because if you do, it will entitle you to the respect you deserve.
Write it down on your notepad.

Others'
The following list of other people's rights will ensure you behave assertively towards them in the discussion. Read them through twice.

They have a right to be treated with respect.
They have the right to be listened to.
They have the right to complain if something's wrong.
They have the right to express anger constructively.
They have the right to be human and make mistakes.
They have the right to make requests of their suppliers.
They have the right to suggest improvement/changes to the system.
They have the right to expect a certain standard of service from us.
They have the right to be advised about changes that we make.

They have a right to use our time to get their problems resolved.

Then choose the one *right* that you need to give others most – because if you do, it will entitle others to the respect they deserve from you. Write it down on your notepad.

Step Four – Self-talk

Below are some of the things that you need to say to yourself in order to programme yourself so that you are able to steer the discussion towards a win:win.

- ■ *"I can acknowledge what they're saying/asking for and get them to acknowledge my/the company's position too."*
- ■ *"I don't have to agree. I can explain what I can and can't do and give my reasons why."*
- ■ *"I can ask them for more time to resolve their issue and tell them when I intend to get back to them."*
- ■ *"I can tell them that I want to treat them fairly and that I want to achieve a satisfactory solution for them."*
- ■ *"I can ask them questions to establish the 'real' issue."*
- ■ *"If we reach a log jam, I can ask what they would consider to be a fair resolution."*
- ■ *"If they get angry, it may not be easy but I can keep calm."*
- ■ *"They do have a right to complain, but not to be abusive towards me."*

Write down below any more self-talk that you believe will help you get the result you want at this meeting or on the telephone.

....
....
....

Finally, choose one piece of self-talk that will be your *mantra* – something you can repeat again and again to yourself as a way of reinforcing your commitment before speaking to them. Write it down on your notepad.

Step Five – Behavioural tips to apply during the discussion
Below is a list of non-verbal and verbal tips to get the result you want. The conversation could be over the telephone or face-to-face.

Non-Verbal tips
Smile when greeting the other person.
Use their name.
Sit in an 'earthed' position, e.g. both feet firmly on the ground.
Keep your gestures open and at waist height.
When asking a question maintain an upright sitting position.
When answering a question take your time, nod thoughtfully before you respond.
Keep a relaxed facial expression.
End your sentences in a lower tone of voice.

Verbal tips
Ask if it's OK to address other people by their first name and use it.
If you've initiated the discussion, ask if they have the time to talk, e.g. *"Margaret, do you have a couple of minutes? I just need further information from you about xyz."*
Signal what you're going to do before you do it, e.g. *"I have a question I'd like to ask"* or *"I'd like to tell you about my idea and get your view."*
Signal that you're looking for a *win:win*, e.g. *"I'm looking for a solution that you'd be sufficiently happy with and one that we can definitely fulfil."*
Ask *open questions* to clarify or get to the root of the problem, e.g. *'What specifically is it that's not working?"*
Test understanding to clarify what's been said, e.g. *"Let me just check that I've understood you correctly. You said that since placing a service call last Tuesday you haven't heard from an engineer and you believe we've forgotten all about you, is that right?"*
Show *empathy* with the customer's situation, this doesn't mean that you have to agree with what they're saying, e.g. *"I can hear that you're upset and that's not a nice way to start the day. Let's see what we I can do to resolve the issue."*
If it's appropriate to say "Sorry" if the error is yours or the company's then say *"I'm sorry"*.
Signal next steps to resolve the situation and be specific about what

you're going to do, e.g. *"I'm going to* request *a visit from an engineer for tomorrow morning. He will call you one hour before he's due to arrive. Then I'll* phone *you at the end of the day to check that everything's OK."* If you agree with something that's being said then say so, e.g. *"Yes I agree, that's what I believe too."*

When disagreeing with the customer reflect what you understand and explain where you differ, e.g. *"You're saying that it's not a practical option for your business. I feel differently: if you try x and y you'll find it solves the problem."*

If the customer refuses to consider your view use a *verbal handshake* in order to open up the possibility of *win:win*, e.g.

"I appreciate your position in that you're really angry because you've had to wait such a long time for an engineer and that you could be losing business as a result. Margaret, do you appreciate that I wouldn't be suggesting this idea if I didn't believe it would solve your immediate problem?"

or

"I appreciate that you think we're very expensive. Do you accept that the service we're offering will save your company thousands of pounds?"

If the customer tries to steer you away from a *win:win* use a 'No' Sandwich, e.g. *"Margaret, I appreciate you think we haven't given you priority and you believe you're entitled to a service rebate. No, that's not the case, we are treating you as a priority and our service records will show this. In the future if there is any lapse in our service, you will be entitled to a rebate."*

If the customer gets angry, demanding and won't calm down or stop ranting, repeat what they're saying to reassure them that you *are* listening before you try to resolve the problem, e.g. *" Mr Davies, I can hear that you're very, very upset and you want to speak with our managing director and until you do you're not going to pay any of our invoices."* **PAUSE** *"I want to help. To do so I need to ask you a couple of questions."* **PAUSE** (only when there is silence will the customer be listening).

If the customer uses abusive behaviour explain that . . .

"I want to help and do the best I can for you. If you continue to use abusive language I will put the phone down. I don't want to do that, so please stop swearing and allow me to help you."

Choose two or three behavioural tips from this list that you believe will work for you. Write them down on your notepad and place this where it will be a continual reminder for you.

CHAPTER 17

FAIR DISCIPLINARY INTERVIEWS

Introduction

In this chapter we provide some helpful guidance about behaving assertively with a member of staff during a disciplinary interview.

For the purposes of this chapter we define a disciplinary interview as a formal meeting that is held on the premises of the workplace, not an external tribunal.

Even in the best-run businesses it may sometimes be necessary to take disciplinary action against employees. Most organisations will have disciplinary rules and procedures to ensure you deal with employees fairly.

Your role may be in HR and the member of staff may not work directly for you. Or it might be one of your own staff who has stepped out of line for the first time, or perhaps it is someone whose behaviour is a consistent problem.

We'd like you to think about a disciplinary interview you may be holding with a member of staff and ask if you feel any of these

Scared that there may be confrontation and things may get out of hand.
Worried that they may turn aggressive and start blaming you.
Full of self-doubt that you may have contributed to the problem.
Anxious that they may become emotional and even start crying.
Concerned that they see things only from their perspective.
Afraid that they might go 'sick' and not turn up.
Irritated because it's always the same with them: they're always quick to blame everyone else but not themselves.

Disappointed because you know they're capable of so much more.
Frustrated because you suspect there is something else going on in their personal life that is affecting their behaviour.
Dissatisfied that things have got this far.
Angry that the employee refused to heed previous warnings.

Do you find yourself saying any of the following?
"Oh no, I remember last time that we spoke he got really aggressive."
"What if they start blaming me and threatening to take me to a tribunal?"
"What if I am partly to blame?"
"She may become tearful. I couldn't cope with that."
"The problem with them is that they don't think about the wider picture."
"I know what will happen: he'll ring in sick and that'll just delay things for another month."
"She always tries to wriggle her way out of it and put the blame on others."
"If only they believed in themselves and stopped making excuses."
"There's got to be something going wrong outside of work but I can't make him tell me."
"Why can't people just do as they're told?"
"Why do I have to get myself emotionally worked up to handle these situations?"

Solution steps - please allow 20 minutes to complete these steps

In order to behave assertively when conducting the disciplinary interview, follow the steps below one by one. You need to allow yourself a quiet solitary 20 minutes to perform these steps today and then a further quiet 20 minutes just prior to the actual interview. Before you start, have a pen and notepad handy.

Step One - Visualising how you want it to be
Imagine in your mind's eye that:
You're conducting a disciplinary interview and it's going well.

......What do you see happening?
......See your posture, facial expression, your gestures.
......Listen to your voice, the tone, particularly the speed and pauses.
......Listen to the tone of the conversation – what is being said?
......See the effect of your assertion on the other person.
......How does that make you feel?

Step Two – Beliefs

The following beliefs will underpin and support your behaviour in the disciplinary interview. Read them through twice.

Assertion isn't about being liked; it's about being respected.
Confrontation can be healthy.
I choose how I behave – I don't have to be manipulated by others.
Nobody makes me feel a particular way; I choose my feelings.
I can be honest *and* respectful in my dealings with others.
I can stand up for myself without attacking people.
I'm responsible for my behaviour; others are responsible for theirs.
We are all capable of change.
Others *are* capable of succeeding.
Facing up to difficult decisions goes with the territory.
I can't always choose the situation but I can choose my behaviour.

Then choose the one that you believe will support you most in the discussion. Write it down on your notepad.

Step Three – Rights

Yours

The following list of rights will provide you with the confidence you need to behave assertively during the disciplinary interview. Read them through twice.

I have the right to formally discipline my staff when necessary.
I have the right to manage my team in the way I believe is fair.
I have the right to say "Yes" or "No" without feeling guilty.
I have the right to support from other managers/HR.
I have the right to expect work of a certain standard from my staff.

I have the right to decide if I want to get involved in solving other people's problems.

I have the right to express my views, which may be different from theirs.

I have the right to express my emotions constructively.

I have the right to be listened to and to be treated with respect.

I have the right to make requests of others.

I have the right to say "No" and refuse unreasonable demands.

Then choose the one *right* that you want to give yourself most – because if you do, it will entitle you to the respect you deserve. Write it down on your notepad.

Others'

The following list of other people's rights will ensure you behave assertively and not aggressively or non-assertively towards them in the disciplinary. Read them through twice.

They have a right to be treated as a human being (not made to look small).

They have the right to know the specific findings of the disciplinary interview and be shown any evidence of poor performance.

They have the right to express their feelings, which may be different from mine.

They have the right to be listened to.

They have the right to question or challenge procedures and decisions.

They have the right to be clear on what is expected of them.

They have the right to sufficient time to make the changes they need to make.

They have the right to ask for help.

They have the right to make mistakes and to learn from them.

They have the right to be given sufficient time to put them right.

They have the right to keep personal information private.

Then choose the one *right* that you need to give others most – because if you do, it will entitle others to the respect they deserve from you.

Write it down on your notepad.

Step Four - Self-talk

Below are some of the things that you need to say to yourself in order to programme yourself for an effective disciplinary interview.

- *"It may not be easy, I can handle it. I've made myself notes and have the supporting evidence."*
- *"I'll speak slowly and clearly, without rushing."*
- *"I can slow down and think before I speak."*
- *"If there is a difficult exchange, I can keep calm."*
- *"If they start to blame me, it may not be easy but I can be firm and have them realise that I'm not a pushover."*
- *"It's OK if they choose to get upset and start crying; I can show respect."*
- *"If they don't seem to care I can explain why they need to accept their responsibilities."*
- *"I can explain the consequences if their behaviour doesn't change."*
- *"I can ask what else they need from me in order for their behaviour to change."*
- *"I can acknowledge any validity in what they say."*
- *"I can disagree and give my reasons."*
- *"They have the right to make mistakes, but need to show a willingness to learn from them."*

Write down below any more self-talk that you believe will help you get the result you want during this interview.

....
....
....

Finally, choose one piece of self-talk that will be your *mantra* – something you can repeat again and again to yourself as a way of reinforcing your commitment before the meeting. Write it down on your notepad.

Step Five – Behavioural tips to apply during the meeting

Below is a list of non-verbal and verbal tips to get the result you want in this disciplinary interview. Ensure that the disciplinary interview is private and uninterrupted.

Non-verbal tips

Use the person's name.

Sit in an 'earthed' position, e.g. both feet firmly on the ground.

Keep your gestures open and at waist height.

When asking a question maintain an upright sitting position.

When answering a question take your time, nod thoughtfully before you respond.

Keep a relaxed facial expression.

End your sentences in a lower tone of voice.

Make eye contact with them.

When things are being resisted you need to be slower in your delivery, your gestures need to be gentler and your posture needs to be open and 'earthed'.

Verbal tips

Follow your company's Disciplinary Guidelines. Typically they will give you guidance on how to start the meeting, e.g.

- describe the exact nature of the complaint with evidence
- make sure any documents you're going to use have been seen by all parties
- allow the opportunity for them to give their point of view
- get all the facts from the meeting and take note of any special circumstances
- summarise what's been discussed and particularly any actions that have been agreed.

If you agree with something that's being said then say so, e.g. *"Yes I agree, that's how I feel too."*

When disagreeing with someone say, *"No, I see it differently in that I believe . . ."*

Test understanding: *"When you mentioned delays did you mean . . . ?"* or signal: *"I'd like to understand more about what you meant when you said . . ."*

Ask *open questions, e.g. "John, what made you decide to take that course of action?"*

If you're interrupted *signal* by saying, *"I'd like to finish what I'm saying."*

If they're not prepared to consider your point of view use a *verbal handshake*, e.g.

"I appreciate your position in that you feel you've been treated unfairly. Do you appreciate my position in that I believe I've treated everybody equally?"

To find out what is bringing about people's strong emotions and behaviour, ask about the wider picture, e.g. *"Paul, I know things haven't been easy for you since we've moved offices. It would be helpful if you could talk about what's really getting to you."*

If things get heated say, e.g. *"Sarah, I don't believe we're making any headway. I suggest we stop now, and come back together at . . ."* or *"Peter, I'm not prepared to continue in this way unless you can give me some specific examples. I would like you to do that so that we can deal with things now."*

Choose two or three behavioural tips from this list that you believe will work for you. Write them down on your notepad and place this where it will be a continual reminder for you.

CHAPTER 18

SUCCESSFUL JOB INTERVIEWS

Introduction

In this chapter we explore the minefield of job interviews.

Many years ago, Suzanne was recruiting salespeople for a large multi-national. She was certainly interested in a particular candidate and continued to ask many searching questions about their background/ experience. After a lengthy barrage of questions from Suzanne the candidate politely asked the question, "I'm curious to find out what exactly is it that you want to know from me, to give you the reassurance that you need, to offer me the job?"

Suzanne realised there and then that this person's ability to 'close' her, was exactly what she was looking for in a salesperson. The job was offered and no more time was wasted.

This situation could be for a promotion/new job at your existing place of work or you could be attending an interview for a position at another organisation.

Prior to the interview we recommend that you investigate the organisation/job role as much as you can. Where possible, find out what it is specifically the interviewer is looking for in a potential employee.

We'd like you to think about a job interview that may be coming up and ask if you feel any of these

Afraid that you're just not going to be able to speak coherently.
Worried that you'll make a fool of yourself.
Nervous that your mind will go blank when answering questions.

Concerned that you may not meet their expectations.
Worried that they may *not* see the 'real' you or that they *will* see the 'real' you and you'll be found out.
Fearful that other candidates are superior to you.
Frightened that you might come across as too desperate.
Afraid that they might think you're under- *or* over-qualified.
Anxious that there may be a 'personality clash'.
Concerned that you may answer their questions too flippantly or come across as arrogant.
Apprehensive about negotiating salary.

Do you find yourself saying any of the following?

"Oh no, I remember the last time I went for an interview I got all tongue-tied and my mind went blank."
"I'll make a fool of myself if I'm not careful."
"I won't be able to answer their questions."
"What if they think I've oversold myself in my CV?"
"What happens if they find me out?"
"I mustn't come across as too keen and I must tone down my enthusiasm otherwise they'll think I'm just desperate to take any job!"
"I won't get the opportunity to show what I can do."
"I'd better not go on and on about what I've achieved because that might scare them and they might feel threatened."
"What if we're totally different and can't see eye-to-eye?"
"I mustn't give careless answers or ask flippant questions and behave like I'm cleverer than them."
"I do hope they're intelligent and don't ask me stupid questions."
"If I ask for what I'm worth, they won't offer me the job."

Solution steps – please allow 20 minutes to complete these steps

In order to behave confidently at a job interview, follow the steps below one by one. You need to allow yourself a quiet solitary 20 minutes to perform these steps today and then a further quiet 20 minutes just prior to the interview.

Before you start, have a pen and notepad handy.

Step One – Visualising how you want it to be
Imagine in your mind's eye that:
You're sitting in a job interview and it's going well.

......What do you see happening?
......See your posture, facial expression, your gestures.
......Listen to your voice, the tone, particularly the speed and pauses.
.......Listen to the tone of the conversation – what is being said?
......See the effect of your assertion on the other person.
......How does that make you feel?

Step Two – Beliefs
The following beliefs will underpin and support your behaviour in the job interview. Read them through twice.

I am a valuable asset to any organisation.
I like myself even though I'm not perfect.
There's no such thing as failure, only feedback.
Respect comes from within, not from without.
I can be honest about my achievements without boasting.
It's OK not to know all the answers.
I have experience and so do others.
We're all different and we're all equal.
My needs are important and so are others'.
I can make things happen, I don't have to wait for them to happen.
My value can be reflected in my salary.

Then choose the one that you believe will support you most in the interview. Write it down on your notepad.

Step Three – Rights
Yours
The following list of rights will provide you with the confidence you need to behave assertively in the interview. Read them through twice.

I have the right to be treated with respect as an intelligent, capable and equal human being.

I have the right to be proud of my achievements.

I have the right to ask for a little more time to think about my answers.

I have the right to correct myself if I make a mistake.

I have the right to say "I don't understand".

I have the right to express my views, which may be different from theirs.

I have the right to challenge and ask questions.

I have the right to ask them for feedback.

I have the right to ask what happens next.

I have the right to ask for what I'm worth.

Then choose the one *right* that you want to give yourself most – because if you do, it will entitle you to the respect you deserve. Write it down on your notepad.

Others'

The following list of other people's rights will ensure you behave assertively towards your interviewer. Read them through twice.

They have the right to know about my career history.

They have a right to the truth.

They have a right to ask for further information.

They have a right to challenge any discrepancies.

They have the right to express their views, which may be different from mine.

They have a right to state their own needs and set their own priorities.

They have a right to choose the best possible candidate for the position.

They have right to say "Yes" or "No" without feeling guilty.

They have the right to change their mind.

They have the right to be treated with respect.

Then choose the one *right* that you need to give others most –

because if you do, it will entitle others to the respect they deserve from you. Write it down on your notepad.

Step Four – Self-talk

Below are some of the things that you need to say to yourself in order to programme yourself for a successful interview.

- *"I can do this."*
- *"I can speak clearly and slowly."*
- *"I've found out many of the questions they're going to ask and I've thought about my answers carefully and made some notes."*
- *"If I don't understand a question, I can say 'I don't understand' and ask for further clarification."*
- *"If they question anything in my CV, I can carefully explain what it means."*
- *"I can be honest about my accomplishments."*
- *"I can tell them what I believe I can contribute to their organisation."*
- *"There may be some differences of opinion on certain subjects; I can acknowledge that different approaches can work."*
- *"I can ask questions about the job role and when they're going to be making a decision."*
- *"I can ask what else they need to know in order to be reassured about my suitability for the role."*
- *"I can negotiate a win:win remuneration package."*
- *"This interview is about whether I meet their specific criteria for the job, not a judgement on me as a person."*

Write down below any more self-talk that you believe will help you get the job.

....

....

....

Finally, choose one piece of self-talk that will be your *mantra* – something you can repeat again and again to yourself as a way of reinforcing your commitment before the interview. Write it down on your notepad.

Step Five – Behavioural tips to apply at the interview

Below is a list of non-verbal and verbal tips to help you perform well at the interview.

Non-verbal tips

Smile when greeting the other person.

Make eye contact with them.

Use the person's name.

Sit in an 'earthed' position, e.g. both feet firmly on the ground.

Keep your gestures open and at waist height.

When asking a question maintain an upright sitting position.

When answering a question take your time, nod thoughtfully before you respond.

Keep a relaxed facial expression.

End your sentences in a lower tone of voice.

Breathe deeply and slowly.

Verbal tips

Before the formal part of the interview begins, ask three *closed questions* to break the ice and encourage an atmosphere of agreement, e.g.

"Cold/warm today, isn't it?"

"Noisy/quiet in here, isn't it?"

"Peaceful/vibrant location, isn't it?"

Test understanding to clarify what's being asked, e.g. *"When you asked about my last experience, what specifically were you interested in?"*

Ask *open questions* to find out more information, e.g. *"I'm curious to find out why the bonus is structured in that way?"*

When describing your achievements place emphasis on the verbs, e.g. "I delivered *a return of . . ."* or *"I rebuilt the whole sector . . ."*.

Place *emphasis* on your measurable achievements, e.g. *"I increased revenue by 50% within 12 months"* or *"I reduced customer complaints by 95% over 2 years."*

Signal if you want to refer back to something, delve deeper or add more, e.g. *"Can I just revisit what you said earlier about . . . ?"*

Give examples to support your point of view, e.g. when asked about your strengths, *"In my last job I was able to withstand the pressure when we were threatened with closure by . . ."*

Show how your weaknesses have helped you develop, give examples, e.g. *"So from that experience I learnt how not to make a assumptions about the future again."*

Negotiate a win:win remuneration package by identifying your minimum salary requirement, what your skills are worth in the current market and your dream salary package (within the bounds of reality). If you disagree on something say, *"I feel differently in that I believe . . ."* instead of the words *"I disagree"*.

Choose two or three behavioural tips from this list that you believe will work for you. Write them down on your notepad and place this where it will be a continual reminder for you.

CHAPTER 19

CONTRIBUTING TO MEETINGS

Introduction

In **Part 1, Chapter 11 'Meeting Behaviours',** we devote a whole chapter to specific *verbal behaviours* to use in meetings and give you the opportunity to become familiar with them. This chapter is about building your confidence so that you can contribute assertively and use these verbal skills.

Most of us spend some part of our day/week in meetings with others. To accurately define a meeting we would say that it is an event where three or more people come together for a minimum of 20 minutes to achieve an objective. Some of these meetings are productive, some definitely aren't, you might even say there are 'the Good, the Bad and the Ugly'!

For some, meetings are a great opportunity to share views and ideas with lots of other people. For others, and you may be one of them, speaking up in front of people is one of the hardest things to do – you may feel that whenever you open your mouth, the spotlight is on you and the pressure just mounts!

You may also find that you can speak more easily when you're surrounded by your peers but when senior management is present you just feel awkward and can't say what you want to say.

Frustration often occurs because meetings aren't well planned – no agendas have been sent out, specific objectives haven't been set and attendees don't know what's expected of them. Also, some meetings proceed just fine because they have a competent chairperson, sadly others lack one and everyone pays the price. All this can be avoided if you pay particular attention to your 'Rights' as a member of a meeting (we'll discuss these later).

We'd like you to think about the meetings that you attend and ask if you feel any of these

Envious of others' ability to articulate so well.

Fear that you're just not able to/or clever enough/or too dim to contribute.

Afraid that people will think you're stupid if you say you don't understand something.

Worried that they might think you're being negative if you don't agree.

Anxious that you may appear confrontational if you question what someone else is saying.

Helpless because you'll spend hours taking minutes but no decisions will be made.

Resentful that your ideas just aren't acknowledged.

Angry that other people don't speak up and contribute more.

Even angrier that some people are allowed to monopolise the meeting with their own agenda.

Resigned to the inevitability that this will just be another waste of everyone's time.

Confused because you don't really know why you're there.

Do you find yourself saying any of the following?

"I don't know what that means, but I can't ask because they'll think I'm stupid."

"It's not fair: they've just got the gift of the gab and I haven't."

"If I don't go along with him on this, he might think I'm just being difficult and take a dislike to me – that won't do my career any good."

"Oh dear, if I ask a question now, I might sound like I'm on the attack."

"Dare I say that with senior management present?"

"Why is it that nobody listens to my ideas?"

"That was a complete waste of time; nobody else had the bottle to say anything!"

"They believe they're so important and they just like the sound of their own voice."

"Here we go again, over and over the same old stuff."

"I'm so bored. This'll be just a complete waste of time."

"Am I supposed to be contributing to this or am I just here to make up the numbers?"

"I hope this ends soon so I can get on with my real work."

Solution steps – please allow 20 minutes to complete these steps

In order to behave assertively in meetings, follow the steps below one by one. You need to allow yourself a quiet solitary 20 minutes to perform these steps today and then a further quiet 20 minutes just prior to the actual meeting. Before you start, have a pen and notepad handy.

Step One – Visualising how you want it to be

Imagine in your mind's eye that:
You're in a meeting and it's going well.

......What do you see happening?
......See your posture, facial expression, your gestures.
......Listen to your voice, the tone, particularly the speed and pauses.
.......Listen to the tone of the conversation – what is being said?
......See the effect of your assertion on the other person.
......How does that make you feel?

Step Two – Beliefs

The following beliefs will underpin and support your behaviour in the meeting. Read them through twice.

I'm only human and so are they.
I can learn from others and they can learn from me.
Everyone has something to contribute.
I'm as important as others; others are as important as me.
I can be honest *and* respectful in my dealings with people.
I can question others without attacking people.
Conflict can be healthy.
My time is important and so is other people's.
I'm responsible for my behaviour; others are responsible for theirs.
Everyone lives in their own unique version of the world.
I can make things happen rather than wait for them to happen.
Meetings can solve problems that individuals can't solve on their own.

Then choose the one that you believe will support you most in the meeting.

Write it down on your notepad.

Step Three - Rights
Yours

The following list of rights will provide you with the confidence you need to behave assertively in the meeting. Read them through twice.

I have the right to say "I don't understand".
I have the right to express my views, which may be different from others'.
I have the right to have my opinions listened to.
I have the right to question/to challenge.
I have the right to agree or disagree without feeling guilty or selfish.
I have the right to change my mind.
I have the right to have some time to think before I answer.
I have the right to express my feelings constructively.
I have the right to an agenda prior to the meeting.
I have the right to know what's expected of me before the meeting.
I have the right to have the meeting stay on track.
I have the right to use my time effectively.
I have the right to ask not to go to the meeting if I feel it's not a good use of my time.

Then choose the one *right* that you want to give yourself most - because if you do, it will entitle you to the respect you deserve. Write it down on your notepad.

Others'

The following list of other people's rights will ensure you behave assertively towards them in the meeting. Read them through twice.

They have the right to express their views, which may be different from mine.
They have the right to be listened to.
They have the right to question/challenge/disagree with me.

They have the right to change their mind.
They have the right to suggest changes/improvements.
They have the right to more time to make a decision.
They have the right to make requests of others.
They have the right to make mistakes.
They have the right to express their feelings constructively.
They have the right to contributions from others.
They have a right to know where I stand.
They have the right to my help to ensure the meeting achieves its aim.
They have the right that I don't waste their time.

Then choose the one *right* that you need to give others most – because if you do, it will entitle others to the respect they deserve from you.
Write it down on your notepad.

Step Four – Self-talk
Below are some of the things that you need to say to yourself in order to programme yourself for a successful meeting.

- *"I know what's expected of me and I've got my views/questions prepared and written down."*
- *"I've been asked to attend so I'm entitled to air my views and be heard."*
- *"If someone says something that I don't understand I can ask them or the chair person to go over it again for me."*
- *"I don't have to go along with them; I can explain what concerns me."*
- *"There'll probably be some differences of opinion; I can stay calm and acknowledge that we see things differently."*
- *"I can put my points across and ask what people think."*
- *"I can ask what else they need from me, to support my view."*
- *"They may want to defend their position quite passionately. If I still feel it's unworkable, I can also say how I feel."*
- *"Senior management are entitled to know what the rest of us think because they want to find the best solution."*

- ▪ *"I can tell them that I'm undecided and that I need more time to consider what they're proposing."*
- ▪ *"If the meeting goes off track I can ask the chairperson to summarise where we are and where we're going."*
- ▪ *"I can invite others to contribute if they don't speak up."*
- ▪ *"I can interrupt someone if they're hogging the limelight and I can suggest that others contribute."*

Write down below any more self-talk that you believe will help you get the result you want at this meeting.

....

....

....

Finally, choose one piece of self-talk that will be your *mantra* – something you can repeat again and again to yourself as a way of reinforcing your commitment before the meeting. Write it down on your notepad.

Step Five – Behavioural tips to apply at the meeting
(also see Chapter 11 'Meeting Behaviours')

Below is a list of non-verbal and verbal tips to get the result you want at this meeting.

Non-verbal tips
Always sit where you have good eye contact with the person who organises or chairs the meeting.
Speak early on in the meeting.
Go back to a point only if you've something new to add.
When addressing someone always use their name.
Let others have their fair share of the overall air time.
Make eye contact with them.
Use firm hand gestures, open and at waist height.
When asking a question maintain an upright sitting position.
When answering a question take your time, nod thoughtfully before you respond.

Breathe slowly and deeply and maintain an 'earthed' position.
End your sentences in a lower tone of voice.

Verbal tips

Agreeing and *Supporting* behaviours are very helpful for you and others and are not controversial, e.g. *"Yes, I agree, Mike, that's how I feel too"* or *"That sounds like an excellent thing to do."*

Before making any contribution *signal* what you're going to do before you do it, e.g. *"I have a question I'd like to ask"* or *"I'm going to agree with you about part of your proposal and explain why I feel differently about another part"* or *"I'd like to tell you about my idea and then invite you to comment."*

Proposing and *Suggesting* behaviours will keep the meeting moving forward, e.g. *"I think we should hire some temporary staff. What do the rest of you feel about that idea?"*

Show that you're listening and appreciate others' ideas by *building* on what they say, e.g. *"Tom, that's a good idea and we could extend this further by . . .".*

Test understanding when you want to clarify something, e.g. *"When you mention problems were you referring to past ones?"* or *"I'd like to understand better what you meant when you referred to . . .".*

Stop interruptions by saying, *"I'd like to finish what I'm saying."*

Signal that you're looking for a *win:win* rather than stick rigidly to your view, e.g. *"I'm keen to get my idea implemented in a way that everyone feels will work for them."*

Invite others to speak by saying, *"I'm interested to find out what you feel about . . ."* or *"I'm curious to know more about your thoughts on . . ."*

When *stating differences* say, *"I see it differently in that I believe . . ."*

State internal feelings when you want to encourage openness and honesty, e.g. *"There's a part of me that wants to agree with you and another part that has some doubt and needs reassuring."*

Choose two or three behavioural tips from this list that you believe will work for you. Write them down on your notepad and place this where it will be a continual reminder for you.

CHAPTER 20

ASKING FOR A PAY RISE

Introduction

In this chapter we consider how you go about asking for a pay rise. Some companies are good at implementing a fair and transparent remuneration policy, whereas others avoid the subject of pay and salary increases like the plague!

We often assume that our manager or the HR department should know that we deserve more money. They should be aware of our needs and expectations and any dissatisfaction we have over our lot. In fact, we even get cross when they appear unconcerned, oblivious, unaware of our efforts and our contribution. We expect people to be mind readers and close followers of our performance and achievements. We can get angry when they're not and often feel sorry for ourselves or resentful towards them.

Some people are great at publicising their achievements, whilst others are worried about blowing their own trumpet for risk of appearing to boast. In this chapter we consider how to promote yourself respectfully to ensure you get noticed and acknowledged for your efforts.

We'd like you to think about a discussion you may be planning to have with your boss/HR, during which you want to raise the subject of your remuneration and ask if you feel any of these

Nervous of asking in the first place.
Fear of rejection.
Concerned that they may not think you're worth it.
Scared they might look for somebody cheaper.
Afraid that they'll think you're being too greedy.
Worried that they'll give you more work/responsibility in return.

Cross because they should know that you're entitled to more.
Unhappy because they just don't seem to care.
Miserable that you're not appreciated enough.
Angry because you know they'll make promises and nothing will happen.
Frustrated the conversation will be a waste of time.
Resentful that you're taken advantage of.

Do you find yourself saying any of the following?
"Oh no, it'll be so embarrassing!"
"What if they say 'No' – I'll feel dreadful."
"They might not think I'm worth it."
"What if they start to look for somebody cheaper?"
"They might expect me to do different shifts; I'd hate that."
"They must know I'm unhappy."
"They must know I'm underpaid."
"Nobody cares about me."
"It'll be like it always is: they'll say 'We'll see' and do absolutely nothing."
"They'll never agree to it so why do I bother?"
"They want me to do more but aren't prepared to pay for it."
"If they don't agree I'll..."

Solution steps – please allow 20 minutes to complete these steps

In order to be confident and assertive when you're asking for a pay rise, follow the steps below one by one. You need to allow yourself a quiet solitary 20 minutes to perform these steps today. Before you start have a notepad and pen handy.

Step One – Visualising how you want it to be
Imagine in your mind's eye that:
You're asking for a pay rise and it's going well.

......What do you see happening?
......See your posture, facial expression, your gestures.
......Listen to your voice, the tone, particularly the speed and pauses.
......Listen to the tone of the conversation – what is being said?

......See the effect of your assertion on the other person.
......How does that make you feel?

Step Two - Beliefs
The following beliefs will underpin and support your behaviour in asking for a pay rise. Read them through twice.

I do not need permission from others to act.
I am a valuable asset to any organisation.
My value can be reflected in my salary.
I can be honest about my achievements without boasting.
I can make things happen rather than wait for them to happen.
When we stand up for ourselves with integrity we gain self-respect and respect from others.
Personal relationships develop more depth when we share our honest reactions and encourage others to do the same.
We get more of what we want when we attend to what others want.
My self-respect comes from me, not from others.
My needs are important; so are theirs.
There's always the possibility of a win:win.

Then choose the one that you believe will support you most in your meeting. Write it down on your notepad.

Step Three - Rights
Yours
The following list of rights will provide you with the confidence you need to ask for a pay rise. Read them through twice.

I have the right to be rewarded appropriately.
I have the right to be proud of my achievements.
I have the right to put across my achievements and describe the value that I'm contributing to the business.
I have the right to be listened to and taken seriously.
I have the right to state my own needs and my own priorities.
I have the right to ask for feedback on my performance.
I have the right to express my views, which may be different from others'.

I have the right to refuse unreasonable requests.
I have the right to take time to consider any proposals put forward.
I have the right to a decision on something that affects me.

Then choose the one *right* that you want to give yourself most – because if you do, it will entitle you to the respect you deserve. Write it down on your notepad.

Others'
The following list of other people's rights will ensure you behave assertively towards them when asking for a pay rise. Read them through twice.

They have the right to be listened to.
They have the right to refuse.
They have the right to give me feedback on my performance.
They have the right to take time to consider my request.
They have the right to express their views, which may be different from mine.
They have the right to suggest changes to the way I work.
They have the right to state their own needs and their own priorities.
They have the right to be human and to make mistakes.
They have the right to treat everyone equally.
They have the right to negotiate with me.

Then choose the one *right* that you need to give others most – because if you do, it will entitle others to the respect they deserve from you. Write it down on your notepad.

Step Four – Self-talk
Below are some of the things that you need to say to yourself in order to programme yourself for asking for a pay rise.

> ■ *"I can ask for a meeting to discuss my remuneration."*
> ■ *"I can express my view calmly and clearly."*
> ■ *"I can explain that I'm looking for a fair pay package and a win:win in respect of business needs."*

- *"I can have other remuneration 'ideas' ready to discuss if my first request is refused."*
- *"I can ask if they acknowledge the contribution I've made to the business."*
- *"I can ask them what else they want from me in order to consider a pay rise."*
- *"I can ask them to be specific rather than accept general comments."*
- *"I can acknowledge that they need time before they make a decision."*
- *"I can accept that they have many different pressures on their time."*
- *"I can accept that they need to be fair across the board when they hand out pay increases."*
- *"If things don't work out, I can acknowledge I did my best."*
- *"I have a choice – I can start looking around at other opportunities."*
- *"I can learn from this experience."*

Write down below any more self-talk that you believe will help you get the result you want.

....
....
....

Finally, choose one piece of self-talk that will be your *mantra* – something you can repeat again and again to yourself as a way of reinforcing your commitment before the meeting. Write it down on your notepad.

Step Five – Behavioural tips to apply when asking for a pay rise

Below is a list of non-verbal and verbal tips to get the result you want at this meeting.

Non-verbal tips
Make eye contact with them.
Use their name.
Find a comfortable seating position in a chair that gives your back support so you can sit upright and be 'earthed'.
Keep your gestures open and at waist height.
Keep a relaxed, open facial expression.
When asking a question maintain an upright position.
When answering a question take your time, nod thoughtfully before you respond.
End your sentences in a lower tone of voice.

Verbal tips
Thank your manager or personnel manager for their time.

Explain your needs and that you're looking for a *win:win*, e.g. *"I'd like to achieve an outcome here, whereby I feel my bonus reflects my efforts and you believe the company's getting value for money."*

Present measurable evidence that shows how your contribution has affected the business results, e.g. *"In expanding our user base by 150%, my team has increased our revenue this year by £50K."*

Give legitimate reasons of how your contribution is worth the sum you're asking for, e.g. *"So I feel it's fair to ask you for my total bonus to reflect the additional service revenue that's been generated."*

Prepare *open questions* on issues you think will be discussed and to find out more information, e.g. *"I'm curious to find out why the bonus is structured in that way."*

Test understanding if you're unsure of what's been said, or you need time to reflect on what's being said, e.g. *"Are you saying that . . . ?"* or *"Is this how you see it?"*

If you feel you're not getting the opportunity to make your point of view, *signal* your intention, e.g. *"Would you like to hear my view on that?'* or *"I'd like to make a comment about that."*

Use a *verbal handshake* when appropriate, e.g. *"Sheila, I get a sense that you think the bonus scheme is fair. Can you see that I wouldn't be asking for you to reconsider mine, if I didn't believe that my contribution was worth a lot more than others?"*

Continue to use language that shows you're looking for a win:win, e.g. *"I want to achieve an outcome that we both feel is fair."*

When you think you need to stand your ground use the *'No' Sandwich*, e.g. *"I can understand you want me to take on this extra responsibility. I am pleased to know you think so highly of me. No, I believe if I take this work, both jobs will suffer as I don't have the time available. How about we look at some alternatives?"*

Place *emphasis* on what you're going to *do*, e.g. *'I'll provide you with the all the evidence you need'* or *"I'll commit to increasing productivity."*
Negotiate a win:win pay rise by identifying your minimum salary requirement, what your skills are worth in the current market and your dream salary package (within the bounds of reality).

Choose two or three behavioural tips from this list that you believe will work for you. Write them down on your notepad and place this where it will be a continual reminder for you.

CHAPTER 21

PRESENTATIONS TO BE PROUD OF

Introduction

In this chapter we show you how to make a presentation that you can look back on and be proud of.

At some point during our working lives most of us find we have to make a presentation to others, either to clients, our peers, senior management, our staff or our shareholders. For some of us this is an event – 'worse than having root canal dentistry without an anaesthetic!'. For others it's not that fearful but it can still be pretty nerve-racking.

To accurately define a presentation we would say that it is an event where you find yourself standing in front of a group of people who are waiting to receive information from you that you believe will benefit them in some way.

Undoubtedly preparation is important, preparation of the material and how best to structure it, so it's memorable and engaging. Equally as important, you need to prepare *yourself* so that you present to your audience confidently and persuasively.

Our aim is to make presentations enjoyable, not terrifying, occasions for you. If you have butterflies at least they will fly in formation.

We'd like you to think about the presentations that you make and ask if you feel any of these

Afraid that others will think you're stupid if you make a mistake.
Worried that you're going to forget everything.
Terrified that someone will ask you a question that you won't know the answer to.

Out of your depth.

Frightened they'll know more than you.

Scared that others will laugh and lose respect for you.

Concerned that you might even lose your job if it goes that badly.

Angry that you have to stand up there in the first place, e.g. why can't others just accept that what you're proposing is the obvious solution, without having to make a 'song and dance' about it?

Resentful that it always falls on your shoulders to make these presentations.

Apathetic because no one's interested and it's a waste of your time.

Do you find yourself saying any of the following?

"Oh it'll be awful: I'll look such a fool."

"What if I go blank like I did last time?"

"They'll think I'm boring."

"I'll look stupid if I don't know the answers."

"They're much cleverer than me."

"They know more than me about the subject and they'll find me out."

"I can see it now - they'll all start sniggering if I mess up."

"This might be the 'nail in coffin' as far as my future's concerned."

"They're so stupid this lot, they wouldn't know a gift horse if it kicked them in the mouth!"

"It's not fair. Why is it always me that's dropped in it?"

"This is a boring subject; no one will be interested."

Solution Steps - please allow 20 minutes to complete these steps

In order to make a confident presentation, follow the steps below one by one. You need to allow yourself a quiet solitary 20 minutes to perform these steps today and then a further quiet 20 minutes just prior to the actual presentation.

Before you start, have a pen and notepad handy.

Step One - Visualising how you want it to be
Imagine in your mind's eye that:
You're making a presentation and it's going well.

......What do you see happening?
......See your posture, facial expression, your gestures.
......Listen to your voice, the tone, particularly the speed and pauses.
.......Listen to the tone of the conversation - what is being said?
......See the effect of your assertion on the other person.
......How does that make you feel?

Step Two - Beliefs
The following beliefs will underpin and support your behaviour in making the presentation. Read them through twice.

This presentation isn't about me. It's about getting my message/material across to people in a way that they understand.
My needs are important and so are other people's.
It's OK not to know all the answers.
I can be honest with my audience and honest with myself.
I can forgive myself for making mistakes and being human.
I can learn from other people and others can learn from me.
There is no such thing as failure, only feedback.
I like myself even though I'm not perfect.
Assertion isn't about being liked, it's about being respected.
You can't please all of the people all of the time.
There are no boring presentations, only boring presenters.
The more I practise, the better I become.

Then choose the one that you believe will support you most in the presentation. Write it down on your notepad.

Step Three - Rights
Yours
The following list of rights will provide you with the confidence you need to make your presentation. Read them through twice.

I have the right to take the time I need to express myself.
I have the right to refer to my notes.
I have the right not to know all the answers.
I have the right to think before I answer.
I have the right to say "I don't know".
I have the right to be treated with respect and be taken seriously.
I have the right to make mistakes sometimes.
I have the right to ask others for help and support if I need it.
I have the right to express my views, which may be different from others'.
I have the right to be honest with people.
I have the right to ask for what I want.
I have the right not to satisfy some people sometimes.

Then choose the one *right* that you want to give yourself most – because if you do, it will entitle you to the respect you deserve. Write it down on your notepad.

Others'
The following list of other people's rights will ensure you behave assertively and not aggressively or non-assertively towards them during the presentation. Read them through twice.

They have the right to question or challenge.
They have the right to express views, which may be different from mine.
They have a right to disagree.
They have the right to ask for information.
They have the right to change their minds.
They have the right to suggest changes.
They have the right to be listened to and taken seriously.
They have the right to be kept informed about future changes that may affect them.
They have the right to ask for what they want.
They have the right to more time to make a decision.
They have the right for me to have prepared properly.
They have the right not to have their time wasted.

Then choose the one *right* that you need to give others most – because if you do, it will entitle others to the respect they deserve from you. Write it down on your notepad.

Step Four - Self Talk
Below are some of the things that you need to say to yourself in order to programme yourself for a successful presentation.

- *"It's only a presentation. I can cope and I can be myself."*
- *"I know my stuff."*
- *"I have done this before. I've learned from that and I can do it again."*
- *"I can breathe deeply and take my time."*
- *"I can look at my notes from time to time so that I stay on track."*
- *"If I do dry up, I can have a glass of water handy."*
- *"I can explain at the start how what I have to say will be useful for them."*
- *"They're only human and so am I."*
- *"I don't need to know all the answers to every question. I can offer to get back to them with the answers."*
- *"I can treat this as a learning opportunity and ask for feedback."*
- *"Their questions might seem pointless to me, but they can still ask them."*
- *"They keep asking me to present because they feel I give value."*
- *"I can make my presentation interesting and informative if I practise beforehand and ensure it's relevant for my audience."*
- *"They want me to do well because I have information they need."*

Write down below any more self-talk that you believe will help you get the result you want at this presentation.

....

....

....

Finally, choose one piece of self-talk that will be your *mantra* – something you can repeat again and again to yourself as a way of reinforcing your commitment before the presentation. Write it down on your notepad.

Step Five – Behavioural tips to apply when making your presentation

Below is a list of non-verbal and verbal tips to get the result you want.

Non-verbal tips

Smile at your audience.

Stand 'earthed' feet forward towards your audience especially when using visual aids.

Slow your breathing down and breathe from low in your diaphragm.

Take a drink of water.

Speak more slowly than you normally would.

Use people's names.

When answering a question take your time, nod thoughtfully before you respond.

Keep eye contact, travel left and right around the room so you make contact with every face.

Keep a relaxed facial expression.

End your sentences in a lower tone of voice.

Keep your gestures open and at waist height.

When someone else is speaking, if you think of a point you want to make, jot it down so that you don't lose it and can continue listening.

When asking a question maintain an *open* upright position.

Verbal tips

Start by introducing yourself and what you want your audience to gain from your presentation, e.g. *"By the end of my talk you will know how to answer the following customer queries/the correct prices to quote/the reasons for the delays in manufacturing/how to grow potatoes/how to fix a leak/how to choose the right colour"*, etc.

Next ask a question, e.g. *"I wanted to start with a question. If there was one particular thing that you wanted to learn more about today what would it be? Please write it down."*

Ask people to tell you and make a note of it so that they can see you have listened and you genuinely want to help.

Gain audience involvement and participation throughout by asking *open* questions, e.g. *"What are your thoughts on this?"*

Test understanding to show you have listened and understood questions, e.g. *"When you asked that question did you mean . . . ?"*

Be honest about what you can answer and what you will have to come back to them about later

Place *emphasis* on what you're going to *do*, e.g. *'I'll email you this before close of business today,"* or *"I'll call you tomorrow about that."*

Summarise at the end the information you have provided and the actions you may have agreed to take.

Check what else people need to know before you finish, e.g. *"If there was something else that you need from me today before we close, what would it be?"*

End on a high by reinforcing key messages with the law of three, e.g.

"So now you know how to:

one – answer those customer queries

two – delight their taste buds

three – guarantee repeat business."

Choose two or three behavioural tips from this list that you believe will work for you. Write them down on your notepad and place this where it will be a continual reminder for you.

CHAPTER 22

ASSERTIVE SELLING

Introduction

In this chapter we focus on how you can develop a customer-centred approach to selling – an approach that allows you to 'close' more regularly, achieve sales more quickly and cost-effectively.

You may be an account manager, work in retail or telephone sales. You may sell to resellers, global organisations or individuals. Whatever type of sales role you hold, you probably have targets to achieve; there may be league tables that compare your results with others and you may have a sales director who continually bangs on about beating the competition.

Remember, while people like to feel in control of their buying decisions they are more likely to buy from people they trust. The best salespeople are the most curious and thorough at establishing their customers' 'real' needs and then convincingly providing them with a solution that meets those needs.

Also remember that people don't buy 'products and services', they buy 'benefits'. A benefit is how the item you're selling can satisfy the customers' 'real' needs, e.g. *to stay looking younger, to save time, to have more flexibility, to feel safer, to have more control, to gain more respect, love, appreciation,* etc. If the benefit achieved is sufficiently compelling to the customer, then they themselves will justify the cost of the product.

Therefore, the key task for the salesperson in a competitive market is to differentiate their company's products and services from the rest of the market so that any difference in price can be justified.

Finally, the old adage – *'If you open the sale right the close is a natural progression'* –couldn't be truer from an assertive perspective and it is with this in mind that we approach our 'Solution' section of this chapter.

We'd like you to think about your approach to your prospective customers and ask if you feel any of these

Uncomfortable in asking them to place an order.

Dread possible rejection.

Fear of being seen as too 'pushy'.

Afraid that they might ring your head office and complain about you.

Wary of criticising the competition in case you might be wrong.

Worried that you're not enough of an 'expert' yet.

Concerned that if you don't agree to extra discount they'll go elsewhere.

Exasperated in your efforts to get through to the correct person.

Irritated when your prospect appears frightened of making a decision.

Angry because you feel taken advantage of.

Do you find yourself saying any of the following?

"I just don't want to sound like I'm desperate."

"I'm dreading this. What if they don't take me seriously, what if they say 'No', . . . ?"

"What if they get aggressive and tell me where to get off?"

"They might even complain about me if I ask them too many questions or chase them up too much."

"If I tell them the truth about our competitor, they might think I'm being devious and resent that."

"They might ask me questions I can't answer – and I'll lose face!"

"If I don't agree to the price they're asking, they'll go elsewhere or they'll always demand the same deal in the future."

"They'll fob me off with the usual excuses."

"They'll lead me on, nod and agree, then buy somewhere else."

"It's not fair. I know they're sitting at their desk, they just don't want to speak to me."

"He's nothing but an idiot this bloke. He's going to cost his company thousands of pounds because he's afraid of taking any risks."
"They always ask for something extra and don't want to pay for it."

Solution steps – please allow 20 minutes to complete these steps

In order to develop an assertive approach to selling, follow the steps below one by one. You need to allow yourself a quiet solitary 20 minutes to perform these steps today and then a further quiet 20 minutes just prior to the actual sales call. Before you start, have a pen and notepad handy.

Step One – Visualising how you want it to be
Imagine in your mind's eye that:
You're in a sales call with a prospective client and it's going well.

......What do you see happening?
......See your posture, facial expression, your gestures.
......Listen to your voice, the tone, particularly the speed and pauses.
.......Listen to the tone of the conversation – what is being said?
......See the effect of your assertion on the other person.
......How does that make you feel?

Step Two – Beliefs
The following beliefs will underpin and support your behaviour in the sales call. Read them through twice.

If you open the sale right, then the close is a natural progression.
People don't buy 'features', they buy 'benefits'.
Enthusiasm is contagious.
People do business with those they trust.
I believe in my company and in my product.
I can question others respectfully.
Rejection of my product or service is not a personal rejection of me.
I can give my view without attacking the competition.
It's OK not to know all the answers.

There's always a potential for win:win.
I can make things happen rather than wait for them to happen.
My needs are important, so are other people's.
We get more of what we want when we attend to what others' want.

Then choose the one that you believe will support you most in the sales call. Write it down on your notepad.

Step Three – Rights
Yours
The following list of rights will provide you with the confidence you need to behave assertively in a sales call. Read them through twice.

I have the right to ask for the business.
I have the right to know whom I'm competing against.
I have the right to ask questions.
I have the right to ask about the decision-making process.
I have the right to suggest changes and improvements.
I have the right to ask about their budgets, timescales, purchasing criteria.
I have the right to share information about my competitors that I believe to be true.
I have the right to say "I do not know. Can I come back to you on that?" because I cannot know everything.
I have the right to refuse unreasonable requests.
I have the right to want to make a profit.
I have the right to negotiate a win:win.
I have the right to use my time effectively.
I have the right to challenge the customers' views.
I have the right to walk away from the sale if it's not profitable.

Then choose the one *right* that you want to give yourself most – because if you do, it will entitle you to the respect you deserve. Write it down on your notepad.

Others'

The following list of other people's rights will ensure you behave assertively, not aggressively or non-assertively towards them during the sales call. Read them through twice.

They have the right to be treated with respect.
They have the right say "Yes" or "No" without feeling guilty.
They have the right to the time they need to make a decision.
They have the right to question/challenge/disagree with me.
They have the right to give feedback.
They have the right to give criticism.
They have the right to ask for the best price.
They have the right to negotiate a win:win.
They have the right to decide to take a different course of action.
They have the right to be illogical in their decision-making.
They have the right to change their mind.
They have the right to not assert themselves.
They have the right to keep information to themselves.
They have the right to ask for what they want.

Then choose the one *right* that you need to give others most – because if you do, it will entitle others to the respect they deserve from you. Write it down on your notepad.

Step Four – Self-talk

Below are some of the things that you need to say to yourself in order to programme yourself for a successful sales call.

- ■ *"I know what I want to talk about and I've got my views/questions prepared and written down."*
- ■ *"I can stay relaxed and keep my voice steady."*
- ■ *"If they say 'No', they're not interested. I can acknowledge this and ask 'What makes you say that?'"*
- ■ *"If they choose not to go ahead, I can ask when would be a good time to make contact again."*
- ■ *"Once I understand their concerns I can put my points across and ask what people think?"*

- ■ *"When I understand their 'real needs' I can explain the benefits and provide them with written/clear evidence."*
- ■ *"I believe that what I'm offering will be useful to their business and help them achieve what they want."*
- ■ *"If they ask me a question I don't know the answer to, I can tell them I'll find out and get back to them."*
- ■ *"I don't have to agree to the discount they're asking for. I can give my reasons; it doesn't have to ruin the relationship."*
- ■ *"I can negotiate on price and achieve a win:win."*
- ■ *"I can ask what else they need from me, in order to place an order."*
- ■ *"I can ask them what stops them buying."*
- ■ *"If they can't speak with me now, I can ask when it would be convenient."*
- ■ *"I know I'm a capable salesperson – I know my stuff."*
- ■ *"I can also ask them for a referral."*
- ■ *"If they ask for additional work to be included, I can charge them a fair price."*

Write down below any more self-talk that you believe will help you get the result you want during this sales call.

....

....

....

Finally, choose one piece of self-talk that will be your *mantra* – something you can repeat again and again to yourself as a way of reinforcing your commitment before the sales call.

Step Five – Behavioural tips to apply in the sales call
Below is a list of non-verbal and verbal tips to get the result you want in this sales call, this could be a telephone conversation or a face-to-face call.

Non-verbal tips
Smile when greeting the other person.
Use the person's name.

Sit in an 'earthed' position, e.g. both feet firmly on the ground.
Keep your gestures open and at waist height.
When asking a question maintain an upright sitting position.
When answering a question take your time, nod thoughtfully before you respond.
Keep a relaxed facial expression.
End your sentences in a lower tone of voice.

Verbal tips
If it's an initial telephone approach check when would be a good time to talk, e.g. *"Hello, I'm Conrad Potts from Teamskills in Sussex. We have a one-day Assertiveness Training Event for Managers next month and I was wondering when might be a good time to talk with you about it?"*

If it's the first face-to-face appointment, ask permission at the start to ask questions, e.g. *"I want to establish if you might benefit from our products, so is it OK to ask some questions and make some notes?"*

Encourage the customer to do most of the talking by asking *open* questions, e.g; *"What? How? Why? When? Who? Which?"*
Test understanding to get clarity, e.g. *"When you mentioned xyz what specifically did you mean?"* or *"I'd like to understand better what you meant when you referred to . . . ?"*

Before you mention the benefits of your product, establish your client's current status and possible unfulfilled 'needs', e.g. *"So I'd like to understand how you operate at the moment?"* Then ask, *"So what would you like to do, that your current system won't allow?"*

If they don't know what else they'd like to do, then ask, *"If you were able to generate xyz in addition how would that help?"* until you generate sufficient interest in the kind of benefits belonging to your product.

Before you mention the benefits *signal* what you're going to *do*, e.g. *"I'd like to tell you about how I think we may be able to help and then I'd like your views."*

Encourage others to speak by saying, *"I'm interested to find out what you feel about . . ."* or *"I'm curious to know more about your thoughts on . . ."*.

If it's an ongoing sale, start the call by *summarising* where you think you are in the sales cycle, e.g. *'Can I just check the status? We agreed to arrange a demonstration of the product and you were going to talk to your colleagues yesterday about a good day for this."*

Ask if anything's changed since you last spoke, e.g. *"What's happened since we last met that might affect things?"*

Use *open* questions to the get commitment, e.g. *"What do you need from me in order to place an order with us today?"* or *"What references would I have to produce in order for you to be fully satisfied that we're the supplier you're going to use?"* or *"What other evidence do you need to reassure you that we're the provider for you?"* or *"What else would we need to offer, in order for you to consider changing supplier?"*

When disagreeing with someone say, *"I see it differently in that I believe . . ."*

Use a *verbal handshake* to achieve agreement on price, e.g. *"I want to offer you the best service deal for your business. Can you see that to provide this level of service we need to charge this amount?"*
Once you've got a "Yes", propose what you believe is fair and ask how they feel about that.

If the customer attempts to knock you further down in price use the 'No' Sandwich to stand your ground, e.g. *"I appreciate you want to do the very best for your company and that budgets are tighter than they've ever been. No, I'm sorry I can't reduce the price any more, because there won't be enough margin in it for us to service your account. Next time you want a keener price, we can look at other options."*

Choose two or three behavioural tips from this list that you believe will work for you. Write them down on your notepad and place this where it will be a continual reminder for you.

CHAPTER 23

HANDLING SENIOR MANAGERS

Introduction

In this chapter we provide you with tips and guidelines about being assertive with senior management.

You may be thinking "I can't do that!"; well don't worry, we won't lead you down a path of self-destruction. We'll just guide you carefully in how to get your points across in a confident way to those individuals who hold more senior positions of responsibility than you do.

For some, 'senior management' is up there on the twelfth floor in the clouds, resident in an ivory tower and detached from the everyday cares and woes of mere mortals. You think they're not going to entertain any ideas that you put forward – or at best they'll treat them in a condescending and patronising way.

It's true that some individuals do possess a 'presence' that the rest of us feel in awe of. When they walk into a busy meeting you can suddenly hear a pin drop. When they step into a lift the other passengers give them more space. We often *choose* to give them more air time, respect and power.

At times like this you may find yourself cross at your inability to converse in a more normal relaxed way. You may find that any attempt at disagreeing fails miserably with you staying quiet or even agreeing.

You can also get fixated with what 'Directors' think of you. You want feedback and perhaps feedback from a person in a position of authority has greater value in your eyes.

Our aim is to help you have a more balanced perspective of the relationship, so that you can have a more relaxed approach and contribute more effectively.

We'd like you to think about discussions and meetings you have with senior management and ask if you feel any of these

Nervous that you may show yourself up.

Anxious that you can't be 'seen' to make a mistake.

Afraid that you're just not going to be able to speak coherently.

Concerned about what they actually think of you.

Afraid they may not like you or think you're stupid.

Anxious that you're not their 'type' and you find it difficult to build rapport.

Worried that they could be bringing in more changes.

Resentful that they're not in your shoes.

Anxious that they think you're trouble.

Scared that any disagreement could be career limiting.

Disengagement, disinterest and apathy.

Do you find yourself saying any of the following?

"Have they noticed me, do they remember me, am I making the right impression?"

"They probably think I'm clever, stupid, interesting, boring, etc."

"If I open my mouth, I may sound stupid and I'll look such an idiot!"

"I won't have the courage to put my own point of view."

"What happens if they find me out?"

"What if we're totally different and can't see eye-to-eye?"

"They might throw their weight around and ruin everything."

"It's up to them if they won't listen; they'll just have to suffer the consequences."

"If I say what I think, they'll believe I'm just being awkward and obstructive."

"Well I'm certainly not going to rock the boat; I've got my bonus to think about."

"They don't care about the troops, so what's the use?"

Solution steps – please allow 20 minutes to complete these steps

In order to behave assertively when you're dealing with senior management, follow the steps below one by one. You need to allow yourself a quiet solitary 20 minutes to perform these steps today and then a further quiet 20 minutes when you can. Before you start, have a pen and notepad handy.

Step One – Visualising how you want it to be
Imagine in your mind's eye that:
You're speaking with senior management and it's going well.

......What do you see happening?
......See your posture, facial expression, your gestures.
......Listen to your voice, the tone, particularly the speed and pauses.
.......Listen to the tone of the conversation – what is being said?
......See the effect of your assertion on the other person.
......How does that make you feel?

Step Two – Beliefs
The following beliefs will underpin and support your behaviour when dealing with senior management. Read them through twice.

They're only human and so am I.
I'm as important as others and others are as important as me.
Everyone has something unique to contribute.
I can make things happen rather than wait for things to happen.
It's easier to ask for forgiveness than seek permission.
My needs are important and so are others'.
When we stand up for what we believe in, we gain respect from others.
It's OK to be me.
They can learn from me and I can learn from them.
I can be honest *and* respectful in my dealings with others.
I can stand up for myself without attacking others.
Assertion is not about being liked, it's about being respected.

Then choose the one that you believe will support you most in your dealings with senior management. Write it down on your notepad.

Step Three – Rights
Yours
The following list of rights will provide you with the confidence you need to behave assertively with senior managers. Read them through twice.

I have the right to deal with others without being dependent on them for approval.
I have the right to judge my own worth.
I have the right to express my own feelings and opinions even if they are different from those of others.
I have the right to be listened to and taken seriously.
I have the right to make mistakes because I'm not perfect.
I have the right to know about decisions that affect me and the overall workings of my department.
I have the right to be clear on what is expected of me.
I have the right to say "I don't understand".
I have the right to ask for what I want.
I have the right to be treated fairly and to be respected.
I have the right to state my own needs and set my own responsibilities.
I have the right to make a contribution.
I have the right to suggest changes to the business.
I have the right to question/to challenge/to disagree.

Then choose the one *right* that you want to give yourself most – because if you do, it will entitle you to the respect you deserve. Write it down on your notepad.

Others'
The following list of other people's rights will ensure you behave assertively and not submissively or aggressively towards senior management. Read them through twice.

They have the right to respect.

They have the right to ask for changes/improvements.

They have the right to make changes that may affect me.

They have the right to change their mind.

They have the right to be listened to and be taken seriously.

They have the right to be kept informed of what's going on.

They have the right to say "Yes" or "No" without feeling guilty.

They have the right not to know all the answers.

They have the right not to satisfy some people sometimes.

They have the right to question/challenge/disagree with me.

They have the right to make requests of others.

They have the right to make mistakes.

They have the right to ask for support from others.

They have a right to our ideas and advice.

Then choose the one *right* that you need to give others most – because if you do, it will entitle others to the respect they deserve from you. Write it down on your notepad.

Step Four – Self-talk

Below are some of the things that you need to say to yourself in order to programme yourself for a successful interaction with senior management.

- *"They may know who I am, or they may not. I can introduce myself when the time is right."*
- *Even if they are important, I can decide calmly what to say and I don't have to be word perfect."*
- *"I can keep things simple and clear and I can leave out less important things."*
- *"They have a million and one priorities and will not be concerned about my accent, dress sense, spelling, etc."*
- *"If they are making changes, I can ask them what they're expecting will happen."*
- *"Their job carries many responsibilities, some I'm aware of and some I'm not."*
- *"They're accountable not just to our customers, but to shareholders and staff."*

■ *"I don't know that they don't care about us; I believe I can get their interest."*

■ *"They don't need to know everything that's going on but they do need to know the important things."*

■ *"I can speak slowly and put my points across in a sensible way."*

■ *"I can be clear and brief and explain the benefits."*

Write down below any more self-talk that you believe will help you get the result you want during this interaction.

....

....

....

Finally, choose one piece of self-talk that will be your *mantra* – something you can repeat again and again to yourself as a way of reinforcing your interaction with senior management. Write it down on your notepad.

Step Five – Behavioural tips to apply when handling with senior managers

Below is a list of non-verbal and verbal tips to get the result you want in discussions with senior managers.

Non-verbal tips

Smile when greeting the other person.

Make eye contact with them.

Keep a relaxed facial expression, nod to show acknowledgement and avoid continuous smiling.

Address them by the name they use to introduce themselves.

Sit in an 'earthed' position, e.g. both feet firmly on the ground.

Keep your gestures open and at waist height.

When asking a question maintain an upright sitting position.

When answering a question take your time, nod thoughtfully before you respond.

Keep a relaxed facial expression.

End your sentences in a lower tone of voice.

Sit or stand where you have good eye contact with the senior manager.

Go back to a point only if you've something new to add.

Verbal tips
If it's an ad hoc discussion, ask if they have the time before you launch into what you have to say, e.g. *"Alan, do you have a couple of minutes now to discuss this?"*

When you're organising a meeting through their PA explain to the PA what impact the meeting will have on the business, e.g. *"I'd like to squeeze 10 minutes into the Director's diary this afternoon so that we can agree the steps for securing the XYZ contract."*

Acknowledge people's time, e.g. *"Thank you for fitting me in. I know you're busy."* Signal what you're going to do before you do it, e.g. *"I have a question I'd like to ask"* or *"I'd like to tell you about my idea and then ask for your thoughts."*

Bring solutions as well as problems, e.g. *"We're experiencing major staff shortages because of sickness. I want to organise temporary staff for the next two weeks and I need your authorisation."*

Prepare *open questions* on issues you think will be discussed, e.g. *"How do you think I can do this differently?"* or *"What leads you to believe that would work better?"* Test understanding when you're uncertain, e.g. *"When you mentioned xyz did you mean . . . ?"*

If you feel you're not getting the opportunity to make your point of view, signal your intention, e.g. *"Would you like to hear my view on that?"* or *"I'd like to make a comment about that."*

Show your appreciation of the bigger picture, e.g. *"This will meet the global /national requirement to hit those all-important targets."*

Place *emphasis* on what you're going to *do, e.g. "I'll provide you with the all the evidence you need"* or *"I'll deliver the presentation in a way that captures their imagination."*

Look for a *win:win* rather than sticking rigidly to your view, e.g. *"You want Tom to lead the project because he's the most senior; I'd like to use Rebecca because she has most experience with the client and is more respected. Are you in agreement?"*

If you agree with something that's being said then say so, e.g. *"Yes I agree; that's how I feel too."*

When disagreeing with them say, *"I see it differently in that I believe . . ."*

Choose two or three behavioural tips from this list that you believe will work for you. Write them down on your notepad and place this where it will be a continual reminder for you.

CHAPTER 24

MANAGING YOUR STAFF

Introduction

In this chapter we focus on how to be assertive with individual members of your staff. We include how to give effective feedback whether it is praise or criticism, and how to encourage their co-operation and commitment to achieve the results you want.

You may have only one member of staff or hundreds. For the purposes of this chapter we refer to those people who report directly to you, e.g. 'direct reports'.

You may have inherited a team or personally recruited each member of your staff. You may have to manage people who are based far away, or your staff may sit next to you in the same office.

There is much written about the art of managing people. One thing that is agreed upon is that different personalities require different styles of management. When you work out what style works best with a certain individual, you can really harness the potential that person has to offer. Some people work best when they're given lots of freedom to get on with their job in their own way. Others work best when they're receiving continuous acknowledgement and feedback. A lack of acknowledgement is usually the reason why people don't co-operate and do their best. Managing those who need lots of acknowledgement can feel exhausting and time-consuming.

Perhaps one of the worst traps we can fall into as managers is to sometimes 'give up' on our staff and end up doing the work ourselves. Good delegation requires you to be able to trust others and trust doesn't come easy for some. The manager's role can also feel lonely and scary at times: you have to make tough decisions and take responsibility for the consequences.

'Patience', 'tolerance' and 'forgiveness' are all words you might associate with counsellors and to some extent you are one of those too. Very often as a manager the person you need to learn to forgive most is *you*.

We'd like you to think about the dealings you have with various members of your staff and ask if you feel any of these

Concerned they may not like you for some reason.

Anxious because you don't know what they're thinking.

Afraid they may react negatively to your feedback.

Worried that they may not think your praise is genuine, or worse, they might relax their efforts.

Scared of any confrontation.

Confused because, unlike you, they're not excited about recent developments.

Hurt, because after all you've done for them, you feel they're taking advantage.

Angry that they don't seem to understand the importance, urgency, critical nature, consequences of their actions.

Irritated because it doesn't matter how many times you tell them, they still keep getting it wrong and you end up having to sort it out yourself.

Frustrated because they won't tell you what the 'real' problem is.

Do you find yourself saying any of the following?

"Oh no, what if I've done something to upset them?"

"They might think I don't rate them or they might think I'm being unfair?"

"I don't want any aggression; I won't be able to handle that."

"If I give them praise, they might slacken off."

"Why aren't they pleased like everyone else?"

"They're just taking advantage of the fact that I'm too soft!"

"After all I've done for them, and they just go and drop me in it like this!"

"Why can't they just get on with things and sort the problem out before things escalate to the Director's office?"

"What have I got to do to get it into their thick skull?"
"Forget them – it's easier to do it myself."
"They expect me to be a mind reader – well I'm not!"

Solution Steps – please allow 20 minutes to complete these steps

In order to behave assertively with a member of your staff, follow the steps below one by one. You need to allow yourself a quiet solitary 20 minutes to perform these steps today and then a further quiet 20 minutes just prior to the actual discussion. Before you start, have a pen and notepad handy.

Step One – Visualising how you want it to be

Imagine in your mind's eye that:
You're talking face-to-face with a member of your staff about an aspect of their work that's been bothering you.
Your discussion with them is going well.

......What do you see happening?
......See your posture, facial expression, your gestures.
......Listen to your voice, the tone, particularly the speed and pauses.
......Listen to the tone of the conversation – what is being said?
......See the effect of your assertion on the other person.
......How does that make you feel?

Step Two – Beliefs

The following beliefs will underpin and support your behaviour in the discussion. Read them through twice.

Assertion is not about being liked; it's about being respected.
I can be honest *and* respectful in my dealings with others.
Praise is far more powerful than criticism.
I can stand up for myself without attacking people.
Confrontation can be very healthy and clears the air.
I can choose how I feel, and others choose how they feel.
I'm responsible for my actions; others are responsible for theirs.

Others are capable of doing a job well.

My needs are important; so are theirs.

Each human being has the potential to change.

Everyone has all the resources they need, even if it takes a little time to find them.

If you always do what you've always done, you'll always get what you've always got.

You get more of what you want when you attend to what others want.

I don't have to lose for other people to win.

Then choose the one that you believe will support you most in the discussion. Write it down on your notepad.

Step Three – Rights
Yours
The following list of rights will provide you with the confidence you need to behave assertively during the discussion. Read them through twice.

I have the right to deal with others without being dependent on them for approval.

I have the right to expect work of a certain standard from my staff.

I have the right to praise and give constructive criticism to my staff about their performance.

I have the right to be listened to and taken seriously.

I have the right to suggest improvements.

I have the right to ask for information and make requests of others.

I have the right to say "Yes" or "No" without feeling guilty.

I have the right to refuse unreasonable requests.

I have the right to change my mind.

I have the right to decline responsibility for other people's problems.

I have the right to more time to make a decision/give an answer.

I have the right to express my emotions constructively.

I have the right to feedback from my staff.

I have the right to make mistakes, because I'm not perfect.

Then choose the one *right* that you want to give yourself most – because if you do, it will entitle you to the respect you deserve. Write it down on your notepad.

Others'
The following list of other people's rights will ensure you behave assertively and not submissively or aggressively towards them in the discussion. Read them through twice.

They have a right to sufficient acknowledgement from me.
They have the right to know what the 'standards of performance' are and what's expected of them.
They have the right to support from me.
They have the right to know what they are doing well and why.
They have the right to constructive criticism, e.g. the impact of their behaviour and what they need to do differently.
They have a right to be treated with respect and dignity and not be made to feel small.
They have the right to express their feelings, which may be different from mine.
They have the right to refuse unreasonable requests.
They have the right to be listened to and be taken seriously.
They have a right to be told in good time about decisions that affect them.
They have the right to make mistakes and learn from them.
They have the right to the necessary time to put mistakes right.
They have the right to get on with their job in their own way once objectives and constraints have been agreed.
They have the right to decide not to assert themselves and accept the consequences.

Then choose the one *right* that you need to give others most – because if you do, it will entitle others to the respect they deserve from you. Write it down on your notepad.

Step Four – Self-talk
Below are some of the things that you need to say to yourself in order

to programme yourself for an effective discussion.

- *"They don't have to like me. It would be nice if they did, but they don't have to."*
- *"There are aspects of their work that they do well and I can be sincere in showing my appreciation for these."*
- *"There are things they need to improve and I can discuss these separately."*
- *"I can be firm and fair in raising any issues that affect their performance."*
- *"Having made some notes I can put my thoughts across and ask what they think."*
- *"If they don't agree with the new structure/processes, I can acknowledge it and explain why they're being introduced."*
- *"There'll probably be some differences of opinion. I can acknowledge that we both see things differently."*
- *"If there is a difficult exchange, I can keep calm."*
- *"If they get upset, it doesn't have to spoil our relationship."*
- *"If they don't seem to care, I can speak to them and explain why they need to accept their responsibility."*
- *"I can say 'No' and give my reasons why."*
- *"They have the right to make mistakes, but not to keep making them."*
- *"I can invite them to suggest how they might change and ask what else they need."*
- *"If they don't tell me what's wrong, I can explain the effects of their current mood on the workload, on me and on others."*

Write down below any more self-talk that you believe will help you get the result you want during this discussion

....

....

....

Finally, choose one piece of self-talk that will be your *mantra* – something you can repeat again and again to yourself as a way of reinforcing your commitment before the discussion. Write it down on your notepad.

Step Five – Behavioural tips to apply during the discussion
Below is a list of non-verbal and verbal tips to get the result you want during this discussion.

Praise is more effective than criticism to improve individual performance and motivation. We **don't,** however, advise you to use praise to 'sweeten the pill' – so that you can say what's really on your mind.

You need to disassociate one from the other so that either praise or criticism is seen as genuine.

Non-verbal tips
Smile when greeting the other person.
Make eye contact with them.
Use the person's name.
Sit in an 'earthed' position, e.g. both feet firmly on the ground.
Keep your gestures open and at waist height.
When asking a question maintain an upright sitting position.
When answering a question take your time, nod thoughtfully before you respond.
Keep a relaxed facial expression.
End your sentences in a lower tone of voice.

Verbal tips
Before giving criticism check that your feedback is specific, e.g. *"What is it that they are doing or not doing that is giving me a problem? How is it affecting their performance, or mine or even others' performance?"*

Help the person tune in to what you want to talk about, e.g. *" Clare, I'd like to talk to you about the weekly meetings."*

Own the criticism with 'I' and describe what they are doing, e.g. *"... because what I've noticed is that you've been arriving late and unprepared."* Show how it affects performance of the business, e.g. *"It makes it difficult for us to make the necessary decisions so everyone can get away on time."*

Invite a response, e.g. *"What causes this/how do you see it?"*

Invite suggestions for change, e.g. *"So how can you organise yourself differently in the future?"*

Test understanding if you're unsure, e.g. *"So are you saying it's the train delays that cause the problem?"*

Confirm the solution, e.g. *"So in future you'll get the earlier train."*

Before making any contribution *signal* what you're going to do before you do it, e.g. *"I have a question I'd like to ask"* or *"I'd like to tell you about my idea and get your view"* or *"I'm unsure about something and thought you might be able to help."*

When you encounter resistance use a *verbal handshake*, e.g. *"I appreciate your position in that you believe it's a stupid idea and it hasn't been tried before. Do you appreciate my position in that I have responsibility for finding a solution to this problem and we're fast running out of time?"*

Signal that you're looking for a win:win rather than sticking rigidly to your view, e.g. *"I'm looking for a solution that we both feel comfortable with."*

If the other person tries to steer you away from a win:win use a 'No' Sandwich', e.g. *"Simon, I appreciate you think that it's none of my business and that you're not upsetting anyone else. No, I've decided that your behaviour needs to change immediately because of the negative impact on team morale. Next time you think I'm wrong, tell me and let's talk about it."*

If you agree with something that's being said, then say so, e.g. *"Yes I agree. That's how I feel too."*

When disagreeing with someone say, *"I see it differently in that I believe . . ."*

When you don't understand something say, *"When you mentioned xyz what specifically did you mean?"* or *"I'd like to understand better what you meant when you referred to . . .".*

Choose two or three behavioural tips from this list that you believe will work for you. Write them down on your notepad and place this where it will be a continual reminder for you.

CHAPTER 25

RELIABLE SUPPLIERS

Introduction

In this chapter we provide you with the necessary building blocks for being assertive with your suppliers.

At some point in our working lives we all find ourselves at the mercy of a supplier. You may be a purchasing manager for a large organisation and travel extensively around the globe, or you may have responsibility for catering or buildings facilities at your place of work. You may run your own business from home and rely on items being hand delivered daily or you may just have a varied experience of dealing with the many utility, IT and telecommunication companies we all come to depend on.

Perhaps the key skill in building successful relationships with suppliers is in your ability to achieve win:win. Sometimes these might feel a million miles away and, anyway, why should you have to be the one who bends over backwards? After all you're the one who's paying the bill!

Building successful relationships in our working lives depends to a large extent in our ability to stand in the other person's shoes and experience the situation from their perspective. Having done that, we find we're better informed and able to choose the most appropriate course of action.

Feeling helpless and powerless when things go wrong can be avoided if we do our best to search for options and realise we have other choices that might work for us.

We'd like you to think about a conversation you may be planning to have with an unreliable supplier and ask if you feel any of these

Manipulated by their salespeople.

Irritated by their engineers' unreliability.

Angered by their help desk's disinterest.

Fed up with their continued broken promises.

Exasperated that no one will take responsibility when things go wrong.

Anxious that they'll miss the deadline and then you'll get the blame from your boss.

Cross because they never let you know what's happening in time.

Powerless because if you change supplier now, it could jeopardise the whole project.

Wary that there may be some hidden clause in the contract, that you overlooked.

Smug because you told everyone it was a bad idea and you've just been proved right.

Do you find yourself saying any of the following?

"That's just typical of salespeople. They promise you the earth but they never deliver the goods."

"I'm getting really fed up with the service we're getting from them. It's just not good enough."

"They never ring you back, nobody passes information on, each time I ring I have to start all over again – it drives me mad!"

"No one ever takes responsibility; it's always someone else's fault."

"They'll trot out the same old excuses."

"They're always dropping me in it like this, making promises but they've got no intention of keeping them."

"If only they'd told me in time, I could have made alternative arrangements."

"If I tell them where to go there'll be a huge gap in supply and I'll get shot!"

"What if they play hard ball and start waving the contract at me!"

"It wasn't my fault. We should never have given them the contract in the first place!"

Solution steps – please allow 20 minutes to complete these steps

In order to behave assertively with your supplier, follow the steps below one by one. You need to allow yourself a quiet solitary 20 minutes to perform these steps today and then a further quiet 20 minutes just prior to the actual conversation.

Before you start, have a pen and notepad handy.

Step One – Visualising how you want it to be
Imagine in your mind's eye that:
You're speaking with this same supplier and it's going well.

......What do you see happening?
......See your posture, facial expression, your gestures.
......Listen to your voice, the tone, particularly the speed and pauses.
......Listen to the tone of the conversation – what is being said?
......See the effect of your assertion on the other person.
......How does that make you feel?

Step Two – Beliefs
The following beliefs will underpin and support your behaviour in the discussion. Read them through twice.

There's more to every business relationship than just price.
When we sacrifice our rights we collude with others to take advantage of us.
You get more of what you want when you attend to what other people want.
I choose how I behave – I don't have to be manipulated by others.
I can make things happen rather than wait for them to happen.
My needs are important, so are other people's.
I don't have to lose for suppliers to win.
I have been a 'push over' in the past'; I can now be assertive.
I can be honest *and* respectful in my dealings with others.
I can stand up for myself without attacking people.
I'm responsible for my behaviour; others are responsible for theirs.

There's always the possibility of a win:win.
Praise gets you more of what you want.

Then choose the one that you believe will support you most in the discussion. Write it down on your notepad.

Step Three – Rights
Yours
The following list of rights will provide you with the confidence you need to behave assertively during the discussion. Read them through twice.

I have the right to expect promises to be kept.
I have the right to be told the truth.
I have the right to be kept informed and consulted about changes that affect us.
I have the right to the terms and conditions being clear and unambiguous.
I have the right to expect work to meet the agreed standards.
I have the right to cancel an arrangement.
I have the right to say "No" without feeling guilty.
I have the right to express anger constructively.
I have the right to be listened to and to be treated with respect.
I have the right to ask for what I want.
I have the right to change my mind.
I have the right to explore other options.
I have the right to complain to a higher authority.
I have the right to get my complaint acknowledged and resolved.
I have the right to achieve a win:win.
I have the right not to satisfy some people sometimes.

Then choose the one *right* that you want to give yourself most – because if you do, it will entitle you to the respect you deserve. Write it down on your notepad.

Others'
The following list of supplier's rights will ensure you behave assertively and not aggressively towards them in the discussion. Read them through twice.

They have a right to be treated with respect.
They have the right to be dealt with in a timely way.
They have the right to question decisions.
They have a right to suggest changes and improvements.
They have the right to make changes to their service.
They have a right to ask for information.
They have the right to be kept informed.
They have the right to be told the truth.
They have the right to be clear on what is expected of them.
They have the right to sufficient time to achieve what's expected of them.
They have the right to make mistakes and be responsible for them.
They have a right to decline responsibility for other suppliers' problems.
They have the right to be listened to.
They have the right to refuse unreasonable requests.
They have right to seek a win:win.
They have a right to encouragement and praise for good service.

Then choose the one *right* that you need to give others most – because if you do, it will entitle others to the respect they deserve from you. Write it down on your notepad.

Step Four – Self-talk
Below are some of the things that you need to say to yourself in order to programme yourself for a successful discussion.

> ■ *"I will give them praise when it's due."*
> ■ *"I can tell them the problems the delays are causing and I can ask them to put things right."*
> ■ *"If they don't seem to care, I can explain why they need to accept responsibility."*
> ■ *"If there is a difficult exchange, I can keep calm."*
> ■ *"I can acknowledge any validity in what they say."*
> ■ *"I can disagree and state my reasons."*
> ■ *"They have the right to make mistakes, but not to keep making them."*

- ■ *"If they start to refer to their contract, I can be firm and repeat my reasons."*
- ■ *"I can explain the consequences if their behaviour doesn't change."*
- ■ *"I can tell them what I'd be satisfied with."*
- ■ *"I can ask to speak with their boss if I don't get satisfaction."*
- ■ *"I can be consistent and persistent in my requests for better service."*
- ■ *"Should I have continued dissatisfaction I can escalate things, e.g. to their MD, my local Trade Association, Ombudsmen, press, my MP, etc."*

Write down below any more self-talk that you believe will help you get the result you want in this conversation.

....

....

....

Finally, choose one piece of self-talk that will be your *mantra* – something you can repeat again and again to yourself as a way of reinforcing your commitment before the discussion. Write it down on your notepad.

Step Five – Behavioural tips to apply during the discussion
Below is a list of non-verbal and verbal tips to get the result you want in this discussion.

Non-verbal tips
Use the person's name.
Breathe deeply. Speak clearly and slowly.
Sit in an 'earthed' position, e.g. both feet firmly on the ground.
Keep your gestures open and at waist height.
When asking a question maintain an upright sitting position.
When answering a question take your time, nod thoughtfully before you respond.
Keep a relaxed facial expression.
End your sentences in a lower tone of voice.

Verbal tips

Acknowledge efforts that people have made on your behalf, e.g. *"Martin, I appreciate how much effort you personally have put in to sort our problem out."*

Signal what you want to talk about today, e.g. *"Martin, what I'm calling about today is to find out why there's been a further delay."*

If they're unwilling to provide a solution, use the following question to stimulate their *creative thinking*: *"There must be a way round this . . .?"*

Pause and wait for them to respond. If they continue to draw a blank ask, *"So if there was a way round this what would it be?"* Be silent and wait.

If you're uncertain about the alternatives offered, ask for more time to consider.

Explain what you'd be satisfied with and why.

If there's still no acknowledgement of your needs use the *verbal handshake* to promote a win:win, e.g. *"I appreciate your position that you feel your hands are tied. Do you acknowledge that the service we've been getting has been poor?"*

If they behave dismissively towards you, point out the discrepancy between what was initially promised and what is now happening, e.g. *"When I first signed the contract I did so on the condition that the goods would be delivered this week. You're now telling me that's unlikely to happen. I'd like you to stand by your original agreement and have them here by the weekend please."* Slow the pace down and use a lower tone of voice as you deliver.

If they continue to ignore your request for help, explain how their behaviour affects you and the business, e.g. *"When you tell me there's absolutely nothing you can do, I feel very angry and let down by your company. The effects of the delay will have a huge impact on our ability to service our own customers and will cost us significant amounts in overtime pay. I don't want to incur this, so please organise a faster delivery time."*

If they still don't satisfy your request explain the consequences, e.g. *'If you don't honour your original agreement, I shall be cancelling the contract/reducing your invoice/charging you for the overtime/talking to your MD/speaking to the Press, etc.* (Choose one only!) *I don't want to*

do that, so please organise what I'm asking for."
Stop interruptions by saying, *"I'd like to finish what I'm saying."*
Finally, you may choose at any time during the proceedings to refer
to the 'relationship' between you and the supplier in order to reach
a win:win, e.g. *"Martin, every month we seem to be having the same
problems. I believe it would be very useful if our respective companies
could find a way of adjusting the framework of our agreement so that
we both enjoy a smoother relationship."*

Choose two or three behavioural tips from this list that you believe
will work for you. Write them down on your notepad and place this
where it will be a continual reminder for you.

CHAPTER 26

WORKING WITH VOLUNTEERS

Introduction

In this chapter we consider how you can prepare yourself to have good working relationships with volunteers. There can be a misconception that because a member of staff is a volunteer they will be totally co-operative all the time and just waiting with baited breath to perform whatever task is ahead of them!

For the purposes of this chapter we define a volunteer as being a member of the organisation who is not on the pay role. They give their services free of charge and agree to abide by the rules of conduct expected by all employees. While you may be thinking of people working for charities, also included in this role are young people performing work experience or, indeed, anyone who for a variety of reasons may be providing their labour free of charge.

You may work for a large charity and rely heavily on the labours of your volunteers or you may work in a small business, which from time to time, offers work experience to pupils at the local school/college. You may be a volunteer yourself and manage a group of volunteers or you may be a member of a voluntary team working alongside paid staff.

Let's take a minute to consider why people perform voluntary work. Suzanne worked as a volunteer for 12 years, on average five hours per week. Her eyes were opened by the different motivations of her colleagues: some wanted to 'give something back', some wanted companionship, some wanted to be noticed, some wanted to change the world. Some wanted a mixture of some or all these things as well as sufficient recognition for their efforts.

Suzanne recalls learning to respect and admire the skilful management administered by one volunteer director of her local group and watched in vain the poor demise another director suffered as a result of a troublesome split between the ranks. She remembers the bitterness felt by some volunteers at their treatment, and the tolerance and patience of others. Suzanne recalls this period of her life to be one of the most rewarding experiences and would thoroughly recommend volunteer work.

We'd like you to think about your relationship with a volunteer who works for you or alongside you and ask if you feel any of these

Scared to upset them in case they just walk out of the door and leave you stranded.

Worried that you've been too heavy-handed in your feedback.

Concerned that what you say may put these young people off working in your particular profession for life.

Afraid they might think that they're not appreciated enough.

Concerned that the new rules from head office will antagonise some volunteers.

Guilty about saying "No" to their requests.

Exhausted because you say "Yes" to all their requests and consequently charge up and down the country attending every fund-raising event they organise.

Uncomfortable that they just like an audience and relish the chance to get on their soap box.

Suspicious that their intentions are not always for the 'greater good' but are actually more self-motivated.

Angry that some volunteers' rebellious actions may cause resistance from your loyal supporters and donors.

Do you find yourself saying any of the following?

"I mustn't upset anyone otherwise I'll have a mutiny on my hands!"
"Oh dear, I hope she doesn't take offence. I was only trying to be helpful in showing her what to do."

"If I don't paint a rosy enough picture, the school will think I'm not serious about helping these kids."

"If I say 'No', they'll think that I don't appreciate their fantastic efforts and that's not true."

"I can see it now: Tim will argue that the changes aren't necessary and stir up resistance among the other committee members and it'll just turn into a bun fight."

"I have to go their event otherwise they'll lose interest and their donations will stop coming and it'll be all my fault!"

"He just likes being in the 'spotlight'."

"She says all the right things but I don't think she means them."

"The problem is that they don't see the bigger picture. We've got to be less aggressive if we want people to listen to us."

Solution steps – please allow 20 minutes to complete these steps

In order to behave assertively with volunteers, follow the steps below one by one. You need to allow yourself a quiet solitary 20 minutes to perform these steps today and then a further quiet 20 minutes when you can. Before you start, have a pen and notepad handy.

Step One – Visualising how you want it to be

Imagine in your mind's eye that:

You're talking face-to-face with a volunteer member of staff or a volunteer colleague about some aspect of their work that's been bothering you.

Your discussion with them is going well.

......What do you see happening?

......See your posture, facial expression, your gestures.

......Listen to your voice, the tone, particularly the speed and pauses.

.......Listen to the tone of the conversation – what is being said?

......See the effect of your assertion on the other person.

......How does that make you feel?

Step Two - Beliefs

The following beliefs will underpin and support your behaviour in the discussion. Read them through twice.

The organisation's standards apply to everybody.
What is fair for one is fair for all.
Assertion is not about being liked; it's about being respected.
I can be honest *and* respectful in my dealings with others.
Praise is far more effective than criticism.
I can stand up for myself without attacking people.
I can choose how I feel and others choose how they feel.
I'm responsible for my actions; others are responsible for theirs.
Each human being has the potential to change.
Others are capable of doing a job well .
Everyone has something useful to contribute.
Healthy disagreements can strengthen relationships.

Then choose the one that you believe will support you most in the communicating with volunteers.
Write it down on your notepad.

Step Three - Rights
Yours

The following list of rights will provide you with the confidence you need to behave assertively when working with volunteers. Read them through twice.

I have the right to give feedback.
I have the right to suggest improvements and changes.
I have the right to expect work of a certain standard from my volunteers.
I have the right to ask them to abide by the rules.
I have the right to have my ideas and opinions listened to, taken seriously and accepted as valid for me.
I have the right to be treated with respect.
I have the right to make requests of others.
I have the right to say "No" without feeling guilty or selfish.

I have the right to make mistakes and learn from them.
I have the right to control the use of my time and my resources.
I have the right to more time to make a decision/give an answer.
I have the right to support from others.
I have the right to have needs that may be different from other people's.
I have the right to be consulted about decisions that affect me.

Then choose the one *right* that you want to give yourself most – because if you do, it will entitle you to the respect you deserve. Write it down on your notepad.

Others'
The following list of other people's rights will ensure you behave assertively and not submissively or aggressively towards them in the discussion. Read them through twice.

They have the right to support from me.
They have the right to know what the standards are.
They have the right to ongoing feedback.
They have the right to be praised for what they do well.
They have the right to a clear picture of what they need to do differently.
They have the right to be treated with respect and dignity and to be their own self.
They have the right to express their feelings, which may be different from mine.
They have the right to refuse unreasonable requests.
They have the right to be listened to.
They have the right to be told about decisions that affect them.
They have the right to make mistakes and learn from them.
They have the right to get on with their task in their own way, once objectives and constraints have been agreed.
They have the right to be different from how others would like them to be.
They have the right to decide not to assert themselves.

Then choose the one *right* that you need to give others most – because if you do, it will entitle others to the respect they deserve from you. Write it down on your notepad.

Step Four – Self-talk
Below are some of the things that you need to say to yourself in order to programme yourself for assertive behaviour.

- *"People do choose to come and work here, knowing there are certain rules."*
- *"I can be honest with these students about what my job is like – the things I like about my job and the things I don't."*
- *"There are many things they do well and I can show appreciation for these."*
- *"There are things they need to improve on and I can discuss these separately."*
- *"If there is a difficult exchange, I can keep calm."*
- *"If they don't agree with the new rules, I can acknowledge that and explain why they're important."*
- *"People can have strong feelings on these things. It doesn't have to spoil our relationship."*
- *"If they can't accept the rules, I can explain the consequences, which may mean they have to leave."*
- *"I can say 'No, I can't attend', give my reasons why and still show them my appreciation of their fantastic efforts."*
- *"They're intelligent people with lots of passion and commitment. I can channel their energies to achieve what we need."*

Write down below any more self-talk that you believe will help you get the result you want from this discussion.

....

....

....

Finally, choose one piece of self-talk that will be your *mantra* – something you can repeat again and again to yourself as a way of reinforcing your commitment before the discussion. Write it down on your notepad.

Step Five – Behavioural tips to apply when working with volunteers

Below is a list of non-verbal and verbal tips to get the result you want when working with volunteers.

Praise is more effective than criticism to improve individual performance and motivation. We **don't** advise you to use praise to 'sweeten the pill', so that you can say what's really on your mind.

You need to disassociate one from the other so that either praise or criticism is seen as genuine.

Non-verbal tips
Smile when greeting the other person.
Make eye contact with them.
Use the person's name.
Sit in an 'earthed' position, e.g. both feet firmly on the ground.
Keep your gestures open and at waist height.
When asking a question maintain an upright sitting position.
When answering a question take your time, nod thoughtfully before you respond.
Keep a relaxed facial expression.
End your sentences in a low tone of voice.

Verbal tips
Before giving criticism check that your feedback is specific, e.g. *"What is it that they are doing or not doing that is giving me a problem? How is it affecting their efforts, or mine or even others'?"*
Signal to help the person tune in to what you want to talk about, e.g. *"I'd like to talk to you about the returns that you've been handling recently."*
Own the criticism with 'I' and describe what they are doing, e.g. *"What I've noticed is that you've been struggling to get things processed in time for collections."*

Show how it affects performance of the team, e.g. *". . . and it makes it difficult for the rest of us to keep tabs on things and we end up duplicating our efforts and wasting time."*

Invite a response, e.g. *"What causes this/how do you see it?"*

Invite suggestions for change, e.g. *"So what help do you need to get things processed in time in the future?"*

When appropriate use a *verbal handshake*, e.g. *"I know you feel the new procedure takes up more of your time. Can you understand, the only way we can make it work is to give it our full commitment?"*

Signal that you're looking for a win:win rather than sticking rigidly to your view, e.g. *"I'm looking for a way forward that we both feel we can work with."*

Be clear when agreeing, e.g. *"I agree. That's the way I feel too."*

When disagreeing with someone use the words *"I see it differently"* instead of *"I disagree"*.

If the other person tries to steer you away from a win:win use a 'No' Sandwich, e.g. *"Angela, I appreciate you'd like me to attend the event you've organised. No, I'm sorry – I've other commitments on that day and I'm not prepared to change them. Next time you're planning a fund-raising event, please give me at least six weeks' notice and if I'm free I'll certainly attend."*

Choose two or three behavioural tips from this list that you believe will work for you. Write them down on your notepad and place this where it will be a continual reminder for you.

CHAPTER 27

FURTHER HELP NEEDED?

There are many ways to develop your confidence and assertion in the workplace. This book may give you the answers you need or you may feel you want further help. This chapter gives you some further ideas on where to get help.

One way is to find a **mentor** – someone whose behaviour you would like to mirror because what they do and say earns them respect from others. Confident people are generally happy to talk about themselves and our experience of people with assertive behaviour is that they're prepared to share their approach and experiences. So, why not speak with your **role model** and ask them if they have a few minutes to talk about, e.g. how they manage to get such and such a person to co-operate with them because you find it difficult. You can learn what other people believe they're entitled to and what they say to themselves just before they act. What you hear might give you the evidence and the reassurance you need to allow yourself to be assertive.

Another approach is to immerse yourself in an **assertive environment.** We've found that there's evidence of plenty of assertion at certain gatherings, e.g. networking business events, your local Chamber of Commerce events, exhibitions of all kinds, adult evening classes, sporting fixtures, charity events, activity holidays, where attendees are excited and passionate about what they're doing and what they hope to achieve. Our motivation drives our behaviour and when we're excited by something we can normally find the confidence to share our thoughts and feelings with others in an assertive way. Other people's assertion can rub off on you because behaviour is catching.

If mixing with others who are assertive is not appealing to you, then you can always purchase one:one **assertive coaching** from a specialist coach, or attend an **assertiveness training programme.** Your organisation may run these events regularly and we strongly advise you book yourself a place.

Alternatively, we run **Assertiveness Training Workshops** throughout the year and you can find out more by looking at our website www.teamskills.co.uk

We would be delighted to see you at one of our **workshops** and help you to gain the respect you're entitled to at work.

In addition to our **Open Workshops** we run **In-Company Events** for all sectors of the workplace. Whether you're a public sector organisation, a large multi-national corporation, a charity or an educational establishment, we can tailor a workshop or speaking event just for you.

We're also keen to hear from you about your experiences in practising assertion, so please feel free to contact our blog at www.teamskills.co.uk

Meanwhile, we wish you the very best in all your endeavours.

Suzanne and Conrad Potts

INDEX